YO SOY LATINA!™

YO SOY LATINA!™

✦

INCLUDES BOTH ORIGINAL OFF-BROADWAY VERSION AND COLLEGE VERSION

Linda Nieves-Powell

iUniverse, Inc.
New York Lincoln Shanghai

YO SOY LATINA!™
INCLUDES BOTH ORIGINAL OFF-BROADWAY VERSION AND COLLEGE VERSION

iUniverse books may be ordered through booksellers or by contacting:

iUniverse
2021 Pine Lake Road, Suite 100
Lincoln, NE 68512
www.iuniverse.com
1-800-Authors (1-800-288-4677)

Professionals and amateurs are hereby warned that the YO SOY LATINA! Off-Broadway version and the YO SOY LATINA! narrative version, being fully protected under the Copyright Laws of the United States of America, is subject to a royalty. All rights including, but not limited to, professional, amateur, recording, motion picture, recitation, lecturing, public reading, radio and television broadcasting and translation into foreign languages are expressly reserved. Inquiries regarding performance rights should be addressed to: Linda Nieves-Powell at latinoflavored@aol.com.

ISBN: 0-595-34145-4

Printed in the United States of America

To all who need a voice.

Contents

Introduction

I haven't always been able to express my Latina pride. Throughout most of my life, I felt I had to hide it to protect myself from people who were threatened by it. When my parents decided to move to the suburbs in Long Island, New York, I had no idea that my wavy black hair and my olive tan complexion would make the Irish kids in the neighborhood react so violently. A few years later my parents moved to Staten Island, New York, a small borough within New York City. The feeling of wanting to fit in didn't change much there, either. I still had to learn a new way of dressing and a new language, if I wanted to hang out with my new Latino friends. But when I didn't fit into their idea of what a Latina was supposed to be, I was again looking for a place to call home. I thought that as I got older, things would change. To my surprise, as I entered the corporate world, again I had to become what other people wanted me to be. I had to follow the corporate dress code and learn the industry-speak in order to become one of them. I had to hide behind another mask, another uniform.

I buried my true self for so long that I forgot who I was supposed to be. I became a chameleon, changing faces to adapt to each new situation. Deep down inside my heart there was a constant yearning: I wanted to feel at home. I was tired of trying to appease everyone—trying to make everyone else feel comfortable while I was compromising myself. I was frustrated with being a shell of a person, not knowing who I was. I wanted to balance my culturally rich world with this other world that seemed not to know—or care to know—anything about me. I needed to find my place.

My soul must have been screaming to the universe for some time, because the strangest thing happened one day while I was trying to write a short monologue for a networking event I had been invited to attend: the hidden, little Latina inside me finally broke loose. She couldn't be kept down; she couldn't be quieted any longer. As I stared at the blank piece of paper in front of me, my soul forced my pen to the paper and began to express itself. It said everything that had been hidden for so long. The anger, the tears, and the humor of this hidden Latina came pouring out onto the page in a powerful stream of emotions. By the end, my soul had claimed its place. It finally was able to exclaim with great pride, "Yo soy Latina!"

And so that is how this journey started: with a simple statement to the world. I guess it was a simple statement to myself. I gave myself the okay to be me—all of me, Latina and American. I no longer felt as though I needed to fit into a category; I created my own category. I'd had no idea that you could do that! Yes, I am Latina, whether I speak great Spanish or not, whether I live in a Latino community or not, and whether I listen to salsa or not. It doesn't matter what anyone else thinks. Ultimately, it's my own sense of identity that defines me.

YO SOY LATINA! is my gift to you. It's not meant for everyone; it's only meant for those who want it. Please accept this gift and learn from it. Empower yourself. And when you have found your own truth, inspire others to do the same.

Linda Nieves-Powell
January 2005

YO SOY LATINA!

✦

(Off-Broadway version)

CAST OF CHARACTERS

Lisette Davila Rivera. *Twentysomething wannabe actress/poet*

Soledad Tejeda. *Dominican; mother of three; divorced; late thirties*

Migdalia Rivera. *Nuyorican; pregnant with second child; married to an African-American man; early thirties*

Jennifer Barriquena. *Nineteen-year-old Chicana college student*

Alicia Blanca. *Colombian; twentysomething; B-list actress; the white Latina*

Maria Elena Gonzalez. *Panamanian; late twenties; the black Latina*

Louisa O'Brien. *Cuban-Irish; corporate attorney; late twenties*

Casting Agent. *Offstage character.*

Note: In the Maria Elena scene, Marisol is played by the Louisa character.

(On a darkened stage, we see a classroom with two windows, a door, and six chairs. On one wall hangs a map of the world; on another wall hangs a poster bearing the words: "Welcome to the 'What is a Latina?' seminar." A light shines from outside a window, and we hear a voice. **Lisette** *enters.)*

Lisette Davila Rivera:

Then fire me! I don't care. But let me remind you: I'm the only one you got that could speak English. Yeah, I thought so, Mr. I-own-one-five-and-dime-store-in-the-worst-section-of-Brooklyn-and-think-I'm-Donald-Trump!

How's he gonna tell me I take too many breaks? Slave trade was over long time ago, Mister Manager!

I ain't no five-and-dime cashier anyway. *Yo soy una actriz,* a future Latina star on the Hollywood Walk of Fame.

I wanna see what you're gonna do when you see me running with the big boys like DeNiro *y* Pacino *y* Garcia.

I'm telling you: as soon as I get that call, the call that will change my destiny, I'm gonna turn my back and I'm never coming back.

Keep your broken-down roach-motel tenements and drug-infested ambitions! That's what I'm gonna be yelling down to you fools when I'm on that 747 to LA. LA. I like that. Imagine me, Lisette Davila Rivera, in LA. "La La Land," the land of dreams. The place where people play Lotto with their lives. I'm gonna be bigger than Rosie Perez, Jennifer Lopez, Salma Hayek, Rita Moreno, and Raquel Welch all put together. I'm gonna be so big that little white kids are gonna wanna be just like me, instead of the other way around.

They're gonna want to know how to dance *salsa y merengue.* They're gonna want to eat rice and beans, *con chuletas y aguacate.* They're gonna want to watch Sabado Gigante for twenty-four hours, like any other bored Latino does on a Saturday night.

I'm gonna turn the whole world on to being Latino!

It's our turn now—our turn to show the world that we're not just little boat people trying to hitch a ride. We got power in our numbers. By the year 2050,

Latinos are gonna rule the world! *(pause)* Well, maybe not "rule," but we will be occupying a hell of a lot of space.

You're gonna be able to pick up a phone book in Wichita, Kansas, and find a million Juan Rodriguezes. You're gonna find Mexicans, Dominicans, Cubans, Puerto Ricans, South Americans on every inch of this planet. We're gonna be everywhere! They're gonna have to make us the primetime television lawyers and doctors on those stupid sitcoms—instead of the Spanglish-speaking maintenance man.

I want to see my face on the TV set for a change. I want to see my olive skin gracing the covers of *Vogue* and *Elle Magazine*. I want to see my *arroz con pollo* thighs inside the *Sports Illustrated* swimsuit issue—not some skinny little waif with bones sticking out of her back that calls herself a supermodel. Let Kate Moss walk through Orchard Beach in the middle of July without getting laughed at.

Bendito nena, put some clothes on; you look like a human wishbone! What's a body without thighs, without a little bit of *sofrito*? Ah? *Yo soy Latina* and proud of it, baby! Nobody's gonna make me feel like an ugly duckling because I'm not anorexic or bulimic.

This is my body, my face—take it or leave it.

And that's what I'm gonna say to Steven Spielberg, and I bet you he'll hire me like that. Why? Because I'm not gonna be afraid to be me. That's right! I'm gonna give my people what they've been wanting for a long time. A chance to see themselves. A chance to feel good about themselves. A chance to free themselves from Brady Bunch reruns. That's right. I watched that show for years, thinking I had the worst parents on the planet. I never saw Mrs. Brady take a *chancleta* to Marcia's head.

I asked Mommy why she didn't act like Mrs. Brady, and you know what she said? She said, "If you don't like the way we live around here, *vete* and take your father with you!"

So for years after that, I fantasized about being a white child in the Brady Bunch house. I pictured Papi coming home from work and hugging me, sitting me on his lap, and telling me how much he loved me. And how proud he was of me just being his daughter. And no matter what I decided to be when I grew up, he would love me regardless.

And then, bam! Reality hits you square in the face. Because the truth of the matter is: there is no Brady Bunch existence for Latinos. Forty million strong, and we're still playing the extra in the Drug-Free America public service announcements instead of the principals in an Ivory Snow commercial.

Kiss my ass! I have the power to be me, not you. I will always be a proud Latina, so that my future son or daughter can grow up confident, self-assured, and proud.

So that they can carry on my love for this beautiful culture of ours. This wonderful array of gifts that have been passed down from our ancestors. A language filled with *sazon*-colored words, exotic foods that feed the hunger of the heart, and music. Oh, that music! Music that makes you stand up and yell:

I am proud to be Latina!

Custom-made gifts that some of us throw away for the sake of becoming accepted into a culture much colder, much less passionate than ours. A culture that looks at our gifts with a sigh of disgust, for fear they will bring down the value of their communities.

Don't move into our neighborhoods! We don't want you here, unless of course you look like us, you act like us, you become us. Forget your past. Join our club. It's free membership! All you gotta do is drain your blood so there are no traces of history left. Forget where you come from! This is your home now! What more can you ask for?

(pause)

Well, Lisette Davila Rivera just wants to feel like she's home. That's what I want. So that I don't have to worry about what you will think of me if I'm sitting in my backyard listening to the congas and timbales on the radio while Willie Colón *y* Tito Nieves *y* Marc Anthony make love to me with their voices. I don't want to have to hide my multicolored family from your homeowner's association. *Tio* Hector *y Tia* Juanita can't help the African, Indian, and European blood that run through their veins.

And neither can I. Let me be who I need to be…

…a proud Latina.

Will you let me do that?

(Lisette *exits.)*

(Lights come up and a young Chicana college student enters the room. She is excited, and she takes a moment to try out a few chairs before picking one that suits her. She sits and looks at the brochure on her seat. She notices that a brochure is on every one of the six seats in the room. A beat later, a young black Latina walks into the room. Somewhat reserved, she nods hello to the young Chicana before taking a seat in the back. Then an older Dominican woman walks in. She looks around the room before taking a seat in front of the black Latina. The door opens again, and in comes the sassy Nuyorican, who makes a beeline to her chair in front of the room. She doesn't say hello to anyone. The door swings open again, and a very colorful and confident Colombian woman enters the room. She is wearing designer sunglasses and is dressed to the nines. The young Chicana smiles and says hello to her, and the Colombian woman brushes it off with a fake hello and a smile. She sashays to a seat far away from everyone. After a few beats...)

Jennifer:

Excuse me, but it does say that this thing starts at three o'clock, right?

Maria Elena:

(checking the brochure again)

Yes. Three o'clock.

Migdalia:

Maybe they got stuck in traffic or something. It took me forever to get out of Westchester.

Alicia:

All I know is: I better be inspired by the end of this thing.

Soledad:

I'm sure you will. This is a wonderful idea. *(looking at **Alicia**)* Excuse me, but you look very familiar.

Alicia:

Don't we all, honey. You know, this is ridiculous. I really hate when people are late. I should've known this would happen.

Migdalia:

Accidents happen.

Alicia:

Well, that's why there's such a thing as a Plan B.

Soledad:

*(to **Maria Elena**)*

Oh, Latinas, we have so much passion!

Maria Elena:

*(to **Alicia**)*

Hey, we've been here this long; we might as well wait a little longer for her.

Jennifer:

(reading from the brochure)

Did you guys see the bottom of this thing? In small print it says: "If the facilitator does not arrive at the scheduled time, please take the following steps."

Alicia:

Great. A self-serve seminar. How Oprah-like.

Migdalia:

There's nothing wrong with Oprah.

Alicia:

I've met Oprah.

Migdalia:

Good for you?

Jennifer:

(quickly intervening)

Look, ladies, we've been here for a while and we're all kind of frustrated at this point. Why don't we at least just introduce ourselves like it says here in the brochure? If she comes, she comes. At least we'll get to know each other.

Maria Elena:

Yes, why don't we do that?

*(**Louisa** walks into the room, talking on her cell phone. The rest of the group watches her as she attempts to finish her conversation.)*

Louisa:

I know. I know. How funny is that? *(laughs)* Listen, I have to go. Yes, yes, we'll talk later. Okay, ciao.

(She closes her cell phone and finally addresses the girls in the room.)

I'm so sorry. The traffic in New York City is the worst. I can never get used to this.

Migdalia:

Told you.

*(During the next several beats, **Louisa**, without knowing she is being watched, prepares herself for the class. She checks her cell phone, takes out a pen, and checks that her lipstick is on. After a beat or two, **Louisa** finally feels the group's eyes on her.)*

Louisa:

I'm sorry; am I supposed to be doing something?

Alicia:

(sarcastically)

No, take your time; we haven't been waiting that long for you.

Louisa:

Oh, you must think I'm the facilitator!

Migdalia:

That's what happens when we assume.

Louisa:

I'm actually here for the same reason you probably are. My apologies; I should have introduced myself when I walked in.

Soledad:

Well, don't worry about it. Good timing, because we were going to begin introducing ourselves like it says here, until the teacher shows up.

Louisa:

Oh, okay.

Jennifer:

*(to **Alicia**, who is listening to messages on her cell phone)*

Do you want to join us?

Alicia:

I guess.

Jennifer:

Okay, I'd like to start. Oh, this is so exciting. Okay, my name is Jennifer Barriquena. I'm nineteen years old. I am a Chicana. I'm from Houston, Texas. When I first got to New York, I was partying like crazy. My parents are Catholic, so leaving home was like escaping a maximum-security prison. I went nuts with all the freedom I got. But after a bunch of silly frat parties and getting drunk and acting stupid, I decided to grow up and get serious. So now I'm doing really well in Latin American history this term. It's my favorite class. Anyway, I think it's about time we come together and do something positive, make a change some-how. All I know is: I'm here because I want to change the world someday.

Migdalia Rivera:

Well, that's very noble of you, mama. I'm not that ambitious. Okay, my name is Migdalia Rivera—a Nuyorican born on the Lower East Side and raised in Brook-lyn! *(She raises her hands up and dances.)* I don't know; I always feel I have to do that when I say Brooklyn. Anyway, I'm a secretary at an investment banking firm. They call me "the crazy Rican." I have to be, 'cause I'm the only Latina in the whole investment banking section. I don't let them get away with shit, and I like it like that. *Que mas?* Oh, I'm pregnant. This is number two for me. I have a little handsome dude that's three years old. I had my first kid when I was twenty-nine, so that makes me a freak in my family. Anyway, I'm not into this whole seminar thing, but I really wanted to know what this "Latina" thing was all about, so that's why I'm here.

Soledad Tejeda:

Hola. My name is Soledad Tejeda; *y soy Dominicana.* I am currently attending college for the first time in my life. I am studying to be a nurse. It's very challeng-ing, but I love it. I have three beautiful girls. Giselle, Lisette, *y* Pasita. Well, Pasita isn't her real name; it's Juanita. But her father decided that he was going to nick-name her after his favorite *tia.* We are no longer together, the father and I. My choice, not his. It was very difficult, but I knew it was what I had to do. Although I am much older than most of you, I feel like I am just starting my life, and so I am afraid, but excited. And I am hoping that I will learn something about myself today. *Gracias.*

Maria Elena Gonzalez:

Hi, girls! My name is Maria Elena Gonzalez, and I am Panamanian. I want to share something with you all. I quit my job yesterday to pursue my lifelong dream. It was such a big decision, but I had to do it. I really want to be an actress. A real actress, not a Chiquita Banana kind of actress. I want to give people some-thing…I don't know…different. So I just took the plunge. I had to. I'm going to work part-time, but hey, these are the sacrifices you have to make, right? Oh, yeah—*(holding up the pamphlet)*—this girl, I've seen her before. I don't know if she's an actress or what, but she does this monologue that kicks ass at the Forty

Second Street subway station. That's why I took it from her. I thought she could teach me a little bit about acting as well. Well, that's my little life story.

*(The girls look at each other to see who will introduce herself next. **Louisa** motions for **Alicia** to go next Alicia stands.)*

Alicia Blanca:

I'm Alicia Blanca. I'm in New York, on location, shooting a movie.

Soledad:

I knew it! I saw you on television.

Alicia:

Yeah, I've done some commercials, nothing major—just some stupid soda commercials that call for a lot of T&A. But hey, work is work. I'm here because I got into a fight with my manager and I thought it would be a good place to hide out. He just pisses me off so bad. I mean, I'm supposed to be getting better movies and more money, but he's like so afraid of taking chances. I mean, please, how am I supposed to become a household name starring in B movies? I didn't spend my father's money so that I could end up like Penelope Ann Miller.

Jennifer:

Penelope Ann Miller?

Alicia:

See? My point exactly. Well, anyway, that's why I'm here. But I'll be honest—I spend my days talking to people who aren't like…I guess…us. I forgot how the other half lives. So, anyway, that's it. *(Alicia sits and quickly stands up again.)* Oh, I'm Colombian.

Migdalia, Louisa, Soledad, Jennifer, and Maria Elena:

(exaggerated, in unison)

Oh!

*(**Alicia** sits, and **Louisa** stands.)*

Louisa O'Brien:

The young girl who gave me this made me really curious. She spoke with such great passion; I tell you, she was either the world's greatest salesperson or the nuttiest person in America. But either way, I really think this is a great idea. So, my name is Louisa O'Brien. I am of Cuban and Irish decent. I am a corporate attorney, and I commute between Miami and New York about four times a year. I am twenty-seven, not married, and currently not looking. I broke up two years ago with my high school sweetheart, and well, it's just been hard finding the right guy. I date, but not seriously anyway. So I'm just taking some quiet time for myself. When I read the flyer, I really liked the idea of talking about our issues—something I don't really get a chance to do that often—so that's why I'm here.

Maria Elena:

*(to **Alicia**)*

Wait a minute, I know where I've seen you. You did that commercial with that boxer, didn't you?

Alicia:

That's me.

Soledad:

You're famous in my house.

Alicia:

Thanks. But enough of me, okay?

Jennifer:

I'm surprised that the teacher is so late.

Louisa:

Well, let's see what the pamphlet says. *(reading from the brochure)* "Welcome, Latinas. You wanted to be brought together to talk about the many issues that concern you as Latinas living in America. You said you were tired of stereotypes, tired of sad stories, confused about the word Latina"—Oh boy, aren't we?—"worried about your future in the world, angry about your misrepresentation in television and film. So, you are here because you have questions you need answered. This is your opportunity to find out things you have always wanted to know about each other and about yourselves. Learn as much as you can about what it means to be Latina. Because until you figure out what it means to you, you will never really be free. And that is what you came here for. You want to be free. Good luck, Latinas."

Migdalia:

I feel like this is gonna be like *Mission Impossible.*

(The girls share a laugh.)

Louisa:

That's weird that it would end off by saying "good luck."

Jennifer:

(with over-the-top enthusiasm)

Well, come on—let's do this!

Alicia:

We're gonna do this seminar by ourselves?

Jennifer:

No, until the teacher gets here.

Louisa:

Great idea. Why don't we just start by asking ourselves questions? You know, things that we would like to know about each other.

(Everyone thinks for a moment, and after a couple of false starts, Louisa speaks up.)

Louisa:

We can't be afraid to ask.

Migdalia:

Okay, I got one. You know what really confuses me? I met two Mexican girls the other day. One says she's Chicana and the other one says she's Mexican. I don't understand what the difference is.

Jennifer:

Oh, that's easy. A Chicana is a person who is definitely an American, but has roots in Mexico and thinks there is a struggle still to be fought. It basically is a person who considers herself a little more active, a little more adamant that there be change along the race/color issues for Mexican-Americans. I consider myself a Chicana because the word Hispanic really irks me. As a person with Mexican ancestry, I feel it is denying my Indian roots. We are not simply Spanish. So for me, the word *Hispanic* is not enough. And *Mexican-American* is an okay term, but I feel that saying I am a *Chicana* means I am striving for change in my community and family. The word *Chicana* lets people know that I am an active participant in this cause.

Soledad:

Interesting, I didn't know that.

Migdalia:

Can I be a Chicana?

Jennifer:

(smiling)

You have to have Mexican roots to be a real Chicana.

Migdalia:

(defensive)

Well, I feel Chicana. I want to take a stand and let people know that things still need to change.

Jennifer:

In the Mexican community or in the Puerto-Rican community?

Migdalia:

Well, in the Latino community, period.

Jennifer:

Chicano is simply for Mexican Americans. Can I be a Nuyorican?

Migdalia:

A Nuyorican is a Puerto Rican born in New York, so I don't think so.

Jennifer:

See.

Migdalia:

Yeah, but it sounds like being a Chicana is more about making a statement.

Jennifer:

Making a statement in the Mexican community. *(with a big smile)* Sorry.

Maria Elena:

I have a question. Why is that whenever someone hears me speak Spanish, they freak out? Like I'm not supposed to know how to speak Spanish.

Alicia:

Obviously because they don't think you're Latin.

Maria Elena:

Why is that?

Alicia:

I don't know.

Migdalia:

'Cause she's black, that's why. Look, I'm married to an African American. I know how that shit works.

Jennifer:

Well, I can understand that. It's the same when people say I don't look Mexican. I mean, what is a Mexican supposed to look like? There are so many different looks that we have; however, everyone assumes that when you look Indian you are a Mexican. But you can look Indian and be from Ecuador or Peru.

Louisa:

People do the same thing to me. Well, Latinas do. They tell me I don't look Latina enough. What does a Latina look like, anyway? How does a Latina speak?

Soledad:

Well, I think a Latina is someone with an olive complexion and dark eyes and dark hair.

Louisa:

So I guess you wouldn't consider me Latina.

Soledad:

I didn't mean that. I mean "typical" Latinas don't look like you.

Migdalia:

What is a "typical Latina"? I love that shit. It's like saying "a typical human being." Who says that there is such a thing as a "typical Latina"?

Jennifer:

Yeah, who started that anyway? I mean, who said that we had to look a certain way.

Maria Elena:

Hollywood, probably. It's amazing that the only way we can become actresses is if we're sexpots. But I'm going to change that.

Alicia:

See, but what you don't understand is that we open the doors for everyone else to come in. Besides, I made a lot of money last year being sexy.

Louisa:

Yes, but that's not the point. People have to know that we embody a lot more than sex.

Migdalia:

It's true, though; how many of us actually look like these chicks in these movies?

Alicia:

Well, it's funny how it's always the average size twelve that has a problem with the way celebrities look.

Migdalia:

I'm pregnant, sweetheart. *(pause)* And when I'm not, I'm a size ten! Don't get it twisted.

Alicia:

Anyway, what bothers me more than anything is the word *Latina*. What the hell does that mean, anyway?

Soledad:

I guess it means a woman who has Latin roots.

Alicia:

Okay, then I guess Italians can be Latina.

Jennifer:

Well, it's better than *Hispanic*. God, that's such an ugly word.

Alicia:

Why can't we just be called Colombian, or Puerto Rican, or Dominican, or Cuban?

Maria Elena:

Doesn't that divide us?

Alicia:

It's ridiculous to think we can all be put in the same pot—and why should I be put in a group, when we all come from different backgrounds?

Louisa:

I don't think there's anything wrong with feeling proud about where you come from. But at the same time we belong to a bigger group, right? Why can't we use both to our advantage?

Alicia:

I think it's impossible to figure out what is going to make us feel "free."

Soledad:

Well, if you think that, then we won't ever find out.

Jennifer:

This reminds me of all these celebs that tell us we have to go to a movie because it's a Latino movie. I'm nineteen years old, I make McDonald's money, and I'm going to a movie that is good, period. So if it happens to be a good Latino movie, then I'm there.

Louisa:

How do you expect Hollywood to change things if you're not willing to support the cause?

Jennifer:

Is the cause paying my tuition? I don't think so.

Louisa:

If the movie was a Mexican movie, wouldn't you go?

Jennifer:

It depends on the movie and who's in it.

Soledad:

How can you change the world if you're not willing to make sacrifices?

Migdalia:

Listen, my husband isn't crazy about Latino movies, and what he likes to watch is way different then what I like. So we have to pick a movie we both agree on and that we think is worth twenty dollars—and not to mention another thirty dollars for the babysitter. I don't care how much money we have in the bank. I've already spent fifty dollars; it better be a damn good movie.

Louisa:

I guess I'm the only one here that feels this way.

Maria Elena:

No, I understand you, Louisa. I go to every Latino movie that comes out. Mind you, most of these movies don't talk about the Panamanian experience, but what matters to me is that I can at least relate to these stories. So I will spend twelve dollars on a ticket, if it means that we'll have more movies about us. Latinos are always complaining that they don't see enough of themselves, but then they don't want to do anything about it. It's about support. They need to put their money where their mouth is.

Migdalia:

I don't think we're gonna agree on everything. We're not the ones that started this problem, anyway.

Maria Elena:

Oh, I think we have a lot to do with it.

Jennifer:

How's that?

Maria Elena:

Tell me right now that we don't all judge each other. And anyone here that says we don't is lying.

Migdalia:

Ooh, I'm with you on that one, girlfriend. Truth be told.

(Migdalia high-fives Maria Elena.)

Alicia:

And what is this so-called truth?

Maria Elena:

That the same prejudices that exist in America exist within the Latino community.

Migdalia:

(to audience)

Well, I hate to be the one to start some shit, but that's true. No disrespect, but I notice that Cubans act really high and mighty.

Louisa:

(to audience)

Great. You know, that's really ridiculous. We get so much flak from certain Latinos because we are an ambitious group of people. If you guys knew more about Cuban history, then maybe you wouldn't feel that way. You know, my great grandfather was a doctor; his brother was an engineer; my aunts were all professionals. They were educated and had their own businesses. As soon as Castro took over private businesses, they left, winding up in Miami to become dishwashers and laborers. Let me ask you this: if you started out professional, why would you settle for anything less?

Migdalia:

(to audience)

Puerto Ricans are just as educated. I have so many cousins that are professionals out there. But instead, everyone says we're the worst of all Latinos when it comes to government assistance.

Louisa:

(to audience)

I guess that's the Cuban's fault.

Jennifer:

(rising and lecturing the women)

It's so funny to me that we sit here and we compare our simple little lives and try to measure which one is better. When you look at our histories, they are very similar. I don't know if you guys are aware of this, but we all had our land taken away from us at one time or another. Most of us had Spaniards dominating our space. That's why we look the way we do. There is not one Latino look, because we truly are mutts. Hell, Spaniards were mutts when they came here to discover new land. They take the land, enslave the native people, bring in the African slaves, intermarry, and rape—and what do you have? A mix of brown people with no real bloodline that they can follow to one heritage. Hello, wake up!

Soledad:

You just started school, didn't you?

Jennifer:

And?

Soledad:

I'm just saying. I know how it feels to have a wealth of new information.

Jennifer:

Sorry, I thought I was teaching you guys something.

Soledad:

Well, I'm just saying that teaching is teaching, and lecturing is lecturing.

Jennifer:

Sorry.

(Jennifer sits.)

Maria Elena:

Look, sweetie, you don't have to impress us with your knowledge. Feel comfortable to be you.

Jennifer:

I'm not trying to impress anyone. I do what I do because I want to do it. I just thought that you guys would find that interesting.

Alicia:

Look, I'm not big on formalities—

Migdalia:

Que sorpresa.

Alicia:

Anyway, why don't we just put it out there? Let's just get to the dirty stuff, because it's gonna happen anyway. Let's just say the things we've heard or have felt about each other's nationalities.

Maria Elena:

That could be dangerous.

Jennifer:

I'm not starting this time.

*(**Louisa**, **Soledad**, **Migdalia**, and **Maria Elena** start looking around the room to place the burden on someone else.)*

Alicia:

Okay, then I'll start. This is only what I've heard. I've heard from other Latinos, of course, that Dominicans are a little lazy.

Soledad:

Oh! Oh! That's why I'm going to school, taking care of three kids, and working a full-time job. It's that lazy gene. I guess that Oscar de la Renta is lazy, huh? Or maybe Julia Alvarez is lazy. You know, she must have been lazy in between *The Garcia Girls* and *In the Time of the Butterflies*. Yeah, that's it. Lazy!

Alicia:

This is simply an experiment, Soledad.

Jennifer:

Well, I'll tell you what I've heard. I've heard that Puerto Ricans are all drug addicts.

Migdalia:

Right, I know. All those drugs that come through the border of Mexico are just to feed those hungry-ass Puerto Rican drug addicts. We really do feel special. By the way, you know what I've heard? That Mexicans hate Puerto Ricans.

Jennifer:

That's not true. Well, I don't think Chicanos do. Mexican-Americans, maybe.

Migdalia:

That's like saying Latinos don't but Hispanics do. Mexican, Chicano, Latino, Hispanic, Nuyorican, Puerto Rican is all the same shit.

Soledad:

Well, Migdalia, I've experienced Puerto Ricans hating Dominicans.

Migdalia:

Claro que si.

Jennifer:

I heard that Central and South Americans hate Mexicans.

Louisa:

Is this what we heard…or believe?

(pause)

Soledad:

You know what else I heard? That Colombians think they're the prettiest women in Latin America.

Jennifer, Migdalia, and Maria Elena:

Oh, please!

Maria Elena:

Look, we all know the things we've heard. Let's try to be bigger than that. The reason I'm here is because I feel like the Invisible Latina.

*(The light changes as **Maria Elena** addresses the audience.)*

You know? The Latina that no one really wants to look at. The Latina that every other Latina wishes would stay away. Hidden. Because I confuse things for you. I make everyone have to stop and think about who they really are and where they come from.

*(We step into **Maria Elena's** youth. She is speaking to **Marisol**, who is played by the actress who plays **Louisa**. All cast members are now ten-year-old girls.)*

Maria Elena:

I'm Farrah! I wanna be Farrah, Marisol! Why do I always have to be Kate Jackson? She's so boring! All she does is complain. And I look like Kate Jackson? You look like Bosley, stupid. And I'm tired of you always telling me who I can marry. I don't like the Osmonds, okay? You could have them. They got big teeth anyway, The Jackson 5 are much cuter. Come on, let me be Farrah. I said, I wanna be Farrah!

Marisol:

I said no!

Maria Elena:

That's so not right, Marisol; you're always Farrah.

Marisol:

You can't even do the flip!

Maria Elena:

Oh yes, I can do the flip. Watch me.

*(**Maria Elena** flips her imaginary blond tresses back.)*

Marisol:

You don't look realistic.

*(**Marisol** runs to her friend, **Migdalia**.)*

Maria Elena:

What do you mean, I don't look realistic? Forget you, then. There's other super-heroes I could be. *(pause)* Aaaah! I know who I can be! I could be *(singing)* Wonder Woman!

*(**Maria Elena** dances around and tries to fly through the air.)*

Migdalia:

Your hips are too big.

Maria Elena:

My hips are not big.

*(**Migdalia** and **Marisol** run to **Soledad**.)*

Maria Elena:

No, wait, okay? Okay? Don't go! I wanna play "Superheroes"! Wait. Give me a second.

Soledad:

Ooooh. I know who you could be. You could be Fat Albert!

Maria Elena:

I don't wanna be Fat Albert. Just wait, I'm thinking. *(pause)* I got it! Oh, I know who I can be. I can be Mestiza: Warrior Princess!

Jennifer:

Who's that?

Maria Elena:

Well, she's not on any channel, but she's famous. She was this beautiful, strong woman. Part African, part Indian. She had radiant dark skin and large hips. Yeah, but she was beautiful. Yup! As a matter of fact, the boys decided to crown her the most beautiful woman in the village, because no one else looked like her. She was so popular that all the girls were so jealous that they tried to bleach her skin white and straighten her hair. She was a great superhero.

Migdalia:

You're making her up.

Maria Elena:

What do you mean, I'm making her up? No, I'm not.

Marisol:

You're stupid!

Maria Elena:

You're stupid!

Marisol, Soledad, Migdalia, Alicia, and Jennifer:

You're stupid!

Maria Elena:

You're stupid. *(She closes her eyes and covers her ears.)* I'm the rubber, you're the glue, whatever you say sticks back to you.

(She opens her eyes. **Marisol, Midgalia, Jennifer, Soledad,** *and* **Alicia** *are no longer there.)*

I wanna play "Superheroes." Don't go…

(speaking to herself)

Maybe I can be somebody else.

*(**Maria Elena** looks into the audience as she pretends to be looking into an imaginary mirror. She touches her hair. She plays with her nose, trying to make it smaller. She looks at the back of her hands, then the front of her hands. After a pause, she returns to the present.)*

Maria Elena:

I didn't have any idols. Everyone told me it was because I was black. I didn't want to be black. I wanted straighter hair. I wanted lighter skin. That little box in my living room told me that I wasn't pretty. That I wasn't normal. I felt invisible. And I still do.

(Lights change. **Maria Elena** *goes back to her seat. Spotlight on* **Alicia** *as she stands.)*

Voice (offstage):

Next!

Alicia:

So I look white. What's the big deal? It's just skin color. When I first started going to auditions, casting directors didn't know what to do with me. You get called out to be in a movie like Carlito's Way, they don't expect you to look like this. Instead, they wind up casting someone who isn't even Latina, but who they think looks Latina. And what people think I should look like is hysterical. And—even more so—the way they think I should speak is even a bigger joke. "Hello, Papi, *mira,* I think you're groovy and shit, and you know, maybe we can get down or somethin' like dat. Whatchu think, Papi *chulito?*" Can I get a break?

I want to be able to tell stories about my people, but they think I don't look typical enough to do that.

Voice (offstage):

Next!

(Alicia runs centerstage.)

Alicia:

Hello?

Voice (offstage):

Your name, please?

Alicia:

Alicia Williams.

Voice (offstage):

I'm sorry; we are looking for Latin types only. Next!

Alicia:

Excuse me. Casting director?

Voice (offstage):

Please, refer to me as "the Voice."

Alicia:

I'm sorry, Ms. Voice.

Voice (offstage):

No, "Voice." Just "Voice."

Alicia:

Oh, excuse me. I'm a little nervous. Voice, I am all Latina; I can assure you that I am. Really. Don't let the name fool you. I also go by the name Alicia Blanca. Williams is my great-great-grandfather's name. See, he was a German Jew—

Voice (offstage):

Then you are not Latina. Next!

Alicia:

Ms. Voice? I mean, Voice. My mother and father are Latino. Really they are. I am one hundred percent Latina.

Voice (offstage):

Can you prove it?

Alicia:

I...I...don't know. I just know that I am.

Voice (offstage):

What is your favorite color lipstick?

Alicia:

Well, I just love lipstick, but if I had to pick one—

Voice (offstage):

Just answer the question!

Alicia:

Neutral Tone by Linda Lee.

Voice (offstage):

Wrong.

Alicia:

Wrong?

Voice (offstage):

The answer is "red." "Red" is what I was looking for.

Alicia:

Okay, if you want me to wear red lipstick for this role, it's no problem. I mean, that's so easy—

Voice (offstage):

No. Next question. What is your favorite television show?

Alicia:

Wow…I mean, there are so many. Well, let me see—

Voice (offstage):

I don't have all day, sweetie!

Alicia:

Sorry. Uh, I would have to say *Frasier*. Yes, *Frasier*.

Voice (offstage):

Wrong!

Alicia:

You don't like *Frasier*?

Voice (offstage):

No, *you* are not supposed to like *Frasier*. The answer was Telemundo. Next question!

Alicia:

Voice?

Voice (offstage):

Yes, Ms. Williams—Ms. Blanca—Ms. Whatever You Are?

Alicia:

I'm sorry, but Telemundo isn't a show. It's a television network.

Voice (offstage):

Ms. Williams, are you questioning the data I have in front of me? This data was compiled by a group of experts in the television industry. Do you hear that? The television industry. We bring reality into your homes. We take our job very seriously and would never mislead the public. We did extensive research on Layteenas. Are you questioning our expertise in this field, Ms. Blanca—Williams?

Alicia:

No, absolutely not. I wouldn't do anything to jeopardize my chance of being cast in the lead for an all-Latino movie. I'm just saying—

Voice (offstage):

Speak Spanish.

Alicia:

Speak Spanish?

Voice (offstage):

Yes, do you understand English?

Alicia:

Yes! I am fluent in English. But I have to be honest with you. I mean, I should have spent more summers with my grandmother, because I really don't know Spanish that well. *Yo hablo poquito. (laughs)*

Voice (offstage):

Oh, Ms. Williams—

Alicia:

(still laughing)

Yes?

Voice (offstage):

I have been so patient—so very patient, don't you think?

Alicia:

(serious)

Well, I guess.

Voice (offstage):

Ms. Williams, do you know how many Latin women who are out there that actually wear red lipstick and speak Spanish?

Alicia:

No, I'm afraid I don't.

Voice (offstage):

They are everywhere! As a matter of a fact, if I looked out my window right now, I would find more than a half a dozen red-lipped, Spanish speaking, hoop-earringed, Spandex-wearing Layteenas. And you know what? I want to find them. Next! Next! Next!

Alicia:

But…but…Look, Voice, I'm really what you want. I've got passion. I love being Latina. I wear Spandex, sometimes. Really. I want to share that with the rest of the world. I want Latinas everywhere to know they should be proud. My cousin from Jackson Heights wears red lipstick. I mean, I am so perfect for this role.

Voice (offstage):

Listen, Ms. Blanca Williams. Just because I am a casting director does not make me insensitive. But right now I need to find the next big Layteena thing. And unfortunately, you're not it. Thank you for your time. Next! Please send me in the next person!

Alicia:

Wait! Look, all right? I don't know what those cards in front of you say, but I'm telling you, the Latina thing is inside me. It's there. I can feel it. I can't explain it. It's just this amazing feeling of pride about who I am. I love who I am. Regardless of my name and the fact that I can't really speak Spanish well. I love that I belong to a beautiful culture that—

(The Voice lets out a big yawn.)

Alicia:

That is so rude.

Voice (offstage):

Excuse me?

Alicia:

That. Yawning like that. You know, maybe the problem isn't me.

(Alicia goes to exit.)

Voice (offstage):

Finally.

(Alicia comes back to centerstage.)

Alicia:

Actually, now that I think about it, the problem isn't me. It's those stupid cards in front of you. Those cards are all wrong, Voice. You and your industry don't know anything about "Layteenas." If you haven't noticed, we Latinas come in so many different flavors that Baskin Robbins is planning to put out a new line. I don't want this ridiculous red-lipstick-wearing job anyway. I don't need to put on Spandex to prove that I am a real Latina. Here, I'll prove to you I'm a real Latina: kiss my *arroz con pollo* ass! Okay, how you like me now?

*(**Alicia** goes to exit again.)*

Voice (offstage):

Ms. Williams!

Alicia:

What?

Voice (offstage):

That was a little too stereotypical—*(pause)*—but I loved it! You got the job!

Alicia:

I've got the lead?

(Alicia walks back towards centerstage.)

Voice (offstage):

You've got the lead. Congratulations, Ms. Williams.

(Alicia runs to centerstage.)

Alicia:

Wow, thank you! Thank you, Voice!

Voice (offstage):

Oh, Voice isn't my real name. It's Ramirez.

*(**Alicia** sits down. Lights come up on **Migdalia** as she is speaking with her mother on her cell phone.)*

Migdalia:

Ma, don't say you don't know. You have to know. This means a lot to me. So let Papi blow a fuse. I don't understand that. I'm Puerto Rican—would it have been okay to bring Bernie Williams home? That's not a different story; it's the same old story. Well, if that's a problem, then we're really screwed. Ay, screwed is not a curse. Look, if you want, I'll tell Papi myself; go ahead put him on the phone; I'll tell him. What's the big deal? I'm a grown woman. Geez, what could he possibly do to me? I'm an adult, for God's sake.

Hi, Papi. *Sí, estoy bien.* Aha, *pue,* I was just telling Mami that I'm really busy, you know. No, I haven't finished my degree yet, but you'll be the first to know when I do. No, I didn't get that promotion either. Well, corporate America is a funny place, Papi. I do work hard. Well, sometimes it's not about how hard you work but who you work for. Look, can we talk about this another time? Well, I want you and Mami to meet someone. Who is he? Well it's not like you know him, it's just someone that means a lot to me. No, he's not Latino. No, he's not Americano. Well, yeah, he's Americano, but not what *you* think is Americano. No, he's not from Mars either, Papi. Well, remember that movie that you liked about that computer thing? Right! It was with Denzel Washington. Well, this guy I'm seeing is like Denzel Washington. What do I mean? I mean he looks like Denzel Washington. I mean, not totally, but they have things in common. No, he's not a movie star. No. No. *(pause)* Well, yeah, he's a little dark. *(long pause)* Papi, he's African American. What do you mean, "what kind?" There's only one kind. He's black, Papi, like Denzel Washington, Spike Lee black. I don't understand why this is an issue. My kids? When we have kids they will be very loved. What am I gonna cook them? I don't know, food. Like what? I don't know, rice and beans, *pasteles,* macaroni and cheese, maybe collard greens. How are beans and greens gonna make them violent? I'm not doing anything to you, Papi. Excuse me? How can you say that word? You don't remember how kids used to call me that? Well, neither is he. Okay, fine, you don't have to meet him. What matters is how I feel, right? Fine. Nobody's as disappointed as me. Yeah. Bye.

(pause)

How do you think I feel, Ma? This is ridiculous. I never expected this from you and him. Ma, I don't know how to tell you this, but I'm gonna have a baby. Ma? Ma? Then talk to me. Don't tell me you have nothing to say! You have a lot to say. I'm having this baby and I'm marrying him and I want you and Papi to give us your blessings. Ma? Ma, don't hang up, please. Mami, don't go! Mami, how can you do this to me? *(phone clicks off)* But I do love you.

(Migdalia *sits, and lights come up on* **Louisa.)**

Louisa:

We can't erase racism. This country was built on racism. Mariposa was five-foot-ten, she was about 175 pounds, and she was the biggest racist in my high school. She was Afro-Cuban and hated anyone that didn't want to be like her. And she hated me. Boy, did she hate me. When she found out I was half-Cuban and half-Irish, I heard that she wanted to "fix" me, whatever that meant. We never spoke; she was in special ed and I was in college-bound, so we never had any classes together. She found out what I was because the student newspaper did a story on biracial students.

So, I'm in the bathroom stall and I hear the front door open. I smell cigarette smoke and I see Mariposa's boots underneath my door. She had her two cohorts with her: a girl from Nicaragua that was living with her tenth foster family and a rich girl from El Salvador who I heard had a crush on Mariposa.

Well, I knew she was waiting for me to come out. So I flush the toilet, and pretend that I don't even see her, and walk past her and her gang of misfits. I hear her laughing. So I dry my hands, and she says, "Hey, Ms. Half-Breed, I wanna talk to you." I didn't even look at her. Look, the girl is an amazon; I would never win. But I had to do something. So I decided I'd try to outsmart her, and I pretended not to hear her. So she walks over to me and looks me in the face and says, "Did you hear me talking?" So I shake my head "no," and I decide to use sign language to make her think I was deaf. So I start doing all these crazy hand gestures, and the Nicaraguan girl says, "I think she's deaf." And Mariposa says, "No shit, Sherlock."

So the girl from El Salvador says, "We could still kick her pretty little ass." And Mariposa says, "How stupid is that? We can't kick her ass if she doesn't know why we're kicking her ass."

And, as luck would have it, the Nicaraguan girl says that she had a foster parent that was deaf and she learned a little sign language while she was there. Now I'm screwed, because I'm not signing with any real communication skill. So she signs and says, "Repeat what you said before." So of course I forgot what I did and I come up with this ridiculous combination of signs I put together from what I saw on commercials and TV shows, and after I was done, Mariposa—who at this point was frustrated as hell 'cause she just wanted to kick butt—asks her cohort what I said.

So the Nicaraguan girl says, "I think she said, 'A sandwich is a sandwich but the mountain is king.'"

I'm laughing like hell inside because I didn't realize that I knew that much sign language. Mariposa has this total confused look on her face and asks, "What the hell does 'a sandwich is a sandwich but the mountain is king' mean?" And the Nicaraguan girl just looked at me strange, then said, "I thought that's what she said. I don't know. Maybe I'm wrong."

And at that point, Mariposa took me by my shirt and pinned me against the cold bathroom wall, and she was so close that we practically touched noses, and that made her El Salvadoran friend a little jealous, because she wound up practically on top of us. And then Mariposa asks if I could read lips, and the pain in my throat made me nod "yes."

And she said, "Well, let me tell you something: I don't like your attitude. It's a little too uppity and white for this school. If you're really half-Latin, then act like you are."

So I have this vision of me dancing the mambo to prove my cultural pride. I didn't know what to do at that point.

I knew that no amount of mambo dancing was going get me out of this mess. And at that very moment the bathroom door opens, Mariposa lets me drop to the floor, and in walks Sylvia, my favorite security guard.

She asks if everything's okay. And Mariposa says, "Yes," but I don't answer, and Sylvia says, "Hey, Louisa, I heard you were trying out for Maria in West Side Story. How'd it go?"

"*Paralyzed*" is not the word to describe what my body felt like at that moment. Then the Nicaraguan girl says, "How's she gonna sing 'I Want to Live in America' if she's deaf?" And it just got deeper and deeper, and I had to speak.

I said, "It went well. Thanks. I'm not sure I'm gonna get it though." Mariposa looked pissed, and the Nicaraguan girl looked like she saw Jesus rise from the dead. And Sylvia says, "Too bad; they always give it to the white girls."

And suddenly time stopped for me. I stood there between Sylvia, a Cuban mom; Mariposa, another Cuban; a Nicaraguan; and an El Salvadoran; and I never felt so out of place. I thought I knew who I was. So my last name is O'Brien and my father is Irish—I can't erase that part of me. And I don't want to. I know my mother's history, and I love that too. I love that I'm two parts of uniqueness, that I have double identity. But to Latinas, I'm just another wannabe.

Well, the recess bell saves the day, and we all walk out behind Sylvia. I thought I had escaped, but Mariposa and her little gang caught up with me and followed me home that same day and actually did manage to kick my butt. I couldn't fight back. Three against a half was too much for me to handle.

(**Louisa** sits. Lights come up on the room. There is an uncomfortable silence. **Jennifer** attempts to break it up.)

Jennifer:

(reading from the brochure)

It says here that we should talk about our favorite foods. Okay, well, I'd have to say *my* favorite food is tortillas.

Migdalia:

Surullos and nice greasy *cuchifritos*.

Soledad:

Puerco asado y platano maduros.

Louisa:

Black beans and rice.

Alicia:

Empanadas.

Maria Elena:

Rice and coconut.

Louisa:

(still reading)

Okay, here's one: "One word that describes you as a Latina." Intelligent!

Jennifer:

Ambitious!

Alicia:

Sexy!

Maria Elena:

Unique!

Migdalia:

Vibrant thang!

Soledad:

Orgullosa! Okay, here's another question. "What do you think about your image in the media?"

Louisa:

I just wish that people could see how resourceful and intelligent we really are.

Jennifer:

Yes, I agree. It really bothers me that we're only seen as whores, drug addicts, welfare recipients, and ignorant. That they think we don't contribute to society.

Maria Elena:

No, this is what I love. There's a commercial with five women who are talking about a feminine product. Four are white. One redhead, two blonds, a brunette...and then they throw one black sister in there. Why can't it be: two black woman, two Latinas, and one white girl?

Migdalia:

I got a better one. For the past ten years, was there ever a Latino on *Friends?* What part of New York City were they living in?

Alicia:

I never noticed that.

Louisa:

Okay, let's go to the next question. "What are your best memories of being Latina?" My *abuela* sitting on her porch drinking *café con leche* and braiding my hair before we went to church.

Jennifer:

The 1994 World Cup; we were so proud to see our flag waving up above.

Maria Elena:

Listening to all my uncles and aunts talk about their childhood.

Alicia:

My mother and father dancing to cumbia on rainy days.

Migdalia:

Going to my cousin's house in the South Bronx. She lived in the projects, and oh, man, how I wished I could live there too. There was always music playing in the halls, people swapping *pasteles* and *coquito*. Now those were parties.

Soledad:

Palm trees and aqua beaches. Brown people with white smiles. Peach-colored houses with little *muchachitos* playing in the street. Warm embraces.

Alicia:

"Sweet Sixteen or *Quinceanera?*" Oh, Sweet Sixteen.

Soledad:

Quinceanera.

Jennifer:

Sweet Sixteen.

Louisa:

Quinceanera.

Maria Elena:

Quinceanera.

Migdalia:

Quinceanera and Sweet Sixteen.

Jennifer:

"What do you want in a man?" Intelligence and compassion.

Maria Elena:

Benecio's eyes, Andy's hair, Benjamin's sexy confidence, Jimmy's physique, and Ruben Blades' voice. Ouch!

Migdalia:

Girl, give me some LL Cool J, licking his lips!

Soledad:

How about a man who's not afraid of a strong woman?

Louisa:

Yes! A man who's not afraid to cry. My ex-boyfriend never cried. He was taught that it wasn't manly to cry. He didn't even cry when we broke up. Bastard!

Maria Elena:

Here's a good one. "Sex education: How did you learn about sex?" Well, sex education for me was they gave me a book about chickens and eggs, and I had to figure it out.

Louisa:

My mother didn't talk about sex. I figured it out when my best friend and I accidentally came across a pornographic magazine called *Creamy Dreams* in her brother's room. We were so sick after that that there was no better birth control.

Migdalia:

My sex education was my mother scaring the hell out of me about pregnancy. She said that the pain is so bad that I would rather die at that very moment then actually have the baby. And my mother had had a cesarean, so I thought that's what everybody had. She showed me her huge scar, and I would go to touch it and she would scream like it still hurt her, and she would say to me, "That's why I don't want you talking to boys right now. This can happen to you."

Soledad:

Basically, my father sat me down when I was fifteen and he said, "Every time you think about kissing a boy, I can feel it. Every time you get curious about knowing more about the boy, I feel it even more. So, if you decide that you want to have sex, I will know exactly when you did it." It took a lifetime to get my father out of my sex life.

Jennifer:

We didn't talk about it. My mother snuck a pamphlet from Planned Parenthood in my room and told me she didn't know where it came from. I knew it was hers. Little did she know I was already on the birth control pill.

Alicia:

My aunt sat me down when I was fourteen. She noticed I had a small hickey on my neck, and she asked me how I got that. I lied and said I didn't know. I told her I thought I bumped into something. She said, "Well, just in case you get clumsy again," and she handed me a condom and a book on birth control methods and told me that a man will tell me anything to get me to page fifteen. So when I read page fifteen, she had circled the man's penis with a red pen and written the words: "The wrong one will ruin your life, but, honey, the right one will too."

Migdalia:

"Something funny about being Latina?" That would be Papi always looking for Latinos in the credits at the end of a movie or TV show. He used to swear that Tom Cruise was really Puerto Rican.

Soledad:

The day my mother's friend tried to do *brujeria* on my father because my mother was worried that my father was having an affair. Two days later, he fell down a flight of stairs and crushed one of his balls. My mother never told him the truth, but she never worried again.

Alicia:

That we yell. Why do we yell when we talk? We could be sitting right next to each other and we still yell!

Maria Elena:

No, better one: that Spanish television has puppets hosting their shows.

Louisa:

Oh, have you ever noticed that Latinos can't say "no" just once? It's like: "No, no, no, no, no, no," or "No *y* no"!

Jennifer:

Oh! What do Latinos do when a plane lands?

(All six girls make the sign of the cross and clap.)

Soledad:

Well, what's really funny to me is that women are the real leaders, the people who don't fear change. We carry the burden of change because men fear change. I know, because I was married to a man that couldn't stand seeing me progress in life.

*(Spotlight on **Soledad**.)*

For twenty years, I woke up next to a man who couldn't wash one dish, never did laundry, and couldn't write out his own checks. It was my job to make sure the house was right for him; it was my job to take care of my kids, forget how I felt. Forget about my needs. He wanted sex, you better give it to him. Whether I was in the mood or not, he wanted access.

I wanted access too: to a different life. I used to see other women go to work in the morning, after I took the kids to school, while I walked back into my nice clean house with nothing to look forward to.

I'll never forget the day I decided to leave. The kids were in school. He was home from work. I watched him sitting in his favorite chair. So comfortable; so at peace. He was reading the newspaper. There was a time that watching him made me feel so safe and secure.

I had just finished cleaning the kitchen, and I looked outside the kitchen window, and for a moment, like a sign from heaven, a beautiful little bird appeared on the ledge. It felt like it was staring at me. It just stood there, like I was.

I looked over at Raul. His world so quiet, and mine was exploding. I felt like the ground was opening up under my feet, and I had to choose my next step carefully. I looked up at the bird, and it was as if it was looking into my soul, and then it just disappeared into the sky. It was a sign. I know it was.

"Raul. Raul. Can I talk to you?" He put down his paper. Almost like he knew something serious was about to happen.

I sit on the sofa beside him and I say, "Raul, I've been thinking about my life lately. There are things I want to do." He says, *"Dime; que tu quiere?"* Men: they think they can fix everything. I tell him I want to go to school. I want to be someone. He tells me I am someone, and goes back to reading his newspaper. I tell him I want to be free, free to experience life. I want to know failure and success. I want to be who I need to be. And in that moment, I saw fire in his eyes, and he slapped me hard against my cheek. There were tears forming in his eyes, and he said, "Soledad, when we got married, we vowed to be together forever. This is something that is sacred to me." I knew it wasn't about sacredness—it was about dependence. He needed me.

Even at that moment, I still wasn't sure of where I was going. My heart was telling me I needed to go; my soul was telling me I needed to find my own way. He cried and asked me if I loved him. I held his head in my lap. I felt his tears rolling down the side of my leg, and I said, "I have loved you, but now I must learn to love myself."

(Lights come up.)

Maria Elena:

Latino men. A good one is hard to find.

Jennifer:

My father's Latino, and he's a good man.

Migdalia:

They're cheaters and liars and lazy. They are still into that stupid machismo shit. And the only ones I see in corporate America are the ones changing light bulbs and pushing a cart.

Louisa:

That's funny; I see engineers, attorneys, and bankers.

Migdalia:

Well, that's not what I see. They're so behind, at this point they're never gonna catch up to us.

Soledad:

The problem is: Latinos still can't get it in their heads that we have a function in life besides being their nurturers and maids. And the funny thing is: we run the show. We are the ones always taking care of everything.

Alicia:

It has a lot to do with the way they're raised, I think. I mean, my mother gave my brother everything. I had to work hard for what I got. They're spoiled. And they expect us to treat them the same way.

Maria Elena:

Okay, in their defense, I'm gonna say that there are good things about being with a Latin man.

Migdalia:

Like what?

Maria Elena:

Like, well, they have a sense of family. Or when you get a joke in Spanish you don't have to explain it—they get it. Or better yet, when you're making love and they tell you they love you it sounds so passionate. *"Ay mami te quiero; te amo."*

Migdalia:

That's disgusting! Let's press the rewind button, please. If they have a sense of family and if they are all that great, then why do they risk it by cheating all the time?

Maria Elena:

You're telling me that every Latino cheats. Shit, I've been with some black men that cheat.

Alicia:

So do white men.

Migdalia:

Yeah, but there are different levels of machismo. Sure, black men have it too, but not at the level that Latinos have it. Latinos have it to the tenth power and then some. Besides, they are so weak. They're corny as hell.

Louisa:

I have friends who are very happily married to Latinos. I just think it's about class and education.

Migdalia:

More power to you. In the meantime, and in between time, I'm very happy with my man.

Alicia:

Migdalia, do you ever wonder why you only like black men?

Migdalia:

Oh, okay. No, I don't. Why don't you break it down for me?

Alicia:

Don't get defensive.

Jennifer:

(to Migdalia)

Did you ever date a white guy?

Migdalia:

Okay, I'll play the game with y'all.

Alicia:

See, that's not right.

Migdalia:

What's not?

Alicia:

"Y'all." What real Latina goes around saying "y'all"?

Maria Elena:

One that grew up down south. I don't think there's anything wrong with that. How many white people go around saying, "Hey, *que pasa?*" That doesn't make them Latin wannabes.

Migdalia:

(to Jennifer)

First of all, let me answer your question. Yes, I have been out with white guys, and honestly I find them bland as hell. They have no personality; they're either way too happy for my taste or have big corks up their asses. Besides, they think we're easy.

Alicia:

I've dated white guys all my life, and I've found them fun and interesting and smart and respectful.

Migdalia:

Well, that's because you like that cork-up-the-ass fun; I don't.

Alicia:

There is something wrong with someone who only dates one nationality.

Migdalia:

Alicia, have you ever dated anyone darker than you?

Alicia:

(hesitantly)

Yes.

Migdalia:

No, you haven't.

Alicia:

At least I date Latinos.

Migdalia:

So, I don't. Does that make me less Latina to you? *(To Maria Elena)* Are you gonna help me out with this?

Maria Elena:

Oh, okay. Well, let's say all of us are sitting in a subway train in New York City. A black guy, a white guy, and a Latin guy get on. Who do you think is going to look at you?

Jennifer:

That's dumb. You have no idea.

Maria Elena:

Oh yes, you do. More than likely, the black guy is going to check out me, Migdalia, and maybe Soledad. The white guy is gonna check out Alicia, Louisa, and maybe Jennifer. The Latino is probably, depending on his skin color, is going to—

Migdalia:

…check us all out!

Maria Elena:

Not all of us. Maybe some of us.

Louisa:

(to Migdalia)

You don't see what you're doing? You're limiting yourself. You haven't experienced other races because you're insecure about yourself.

Jennifer:

Here's the reality, people: guys, no matter what color, love beautiful women. Period!

Migdalia:

Fine, but there is still a racial issue here. Besides, white guys don't usually go gaga over someone like me. They couldn't handle me anyway!

(Migdalia high-fives Maria Elena.)

Louisa:

That's not true. White guys love Latinas.

Migdalia:

Well, that's because you're offering them a watered-down version.

(The girls freeze.)

Louisa:

Excuse me?

Migdalia:

I'm just saying, it's not like you're a—

Louisa:

...a real Latina?

Migdalia:

I didn't say that. You did.

Louisa:

Well, I can't help it. If you're a lot like your father—

Migdalia:

And your Irish father didn't have a problem with Latinos?

Louisa:

He was married to my mother.

Migdalia:

Was? So where is he now?

Louisa:

That doesn't have anything to do with his character. Unlike your father, who was so confused as to who he was that he created self-hatred in you. The reason you can't stand a Latino man is because you can't stand yourself.

(Migdalia stands.)

Migdalia:

(angrily)

You don't know me, Ms. Cuban, half-Irish wannabe.

Alicia:

If she's a wannabe, then you're a wannabe.

Migdalia:

Nobody's more a wannabe than an actress who has to change her name.

Alicia:

I changed my name for business reasons.

Migdalia:

You changed your name so you could hide the fact that you are Latin.

Jennifer:

She changed her name to get work.

(Maria Elena stands.)

Maria Elena:

Well, how funny is that? I can't change my name, because no matter what I change it to, I'm still black.

Jennifer:

I don't understand what we're doing here. I'm not feeling any freer.

Maria Elena:

Yeah, how is all of this supposed to be helping us be free?

Migdalia:

You know, Latinos are always bitching about how they want to come together and unite, and y'all just don't know how to do that. It's not gonna happen, because a lot of you are not being real with yourselves.

Maria Elena:

Real in what way, Migdalia?

Migdalia:

If there was a million-man march for Latinos in Washington, how many of us would actually pick ourselves up to go? Most of us would be sitting our asses in front of the television talking about how Latinos should just be quiet and leave shit alone, while the other ten of us march for equal rights. That's how it's always been and that's how it's gonna be. We come in too many different colors, too many different backgrounds, from the ghetto and from the suburbs. Unity ain't happening here.

Louisa:

Okay, Migdalia, maybe unity won't happen for a while, but we have to believe that every step we take is going to help us out. We can't just sit around and worry about the people who don't want to get involved. I fight for people's rights every day. I know what it takes to win a fight. The only way to move forward is to take risks.

Migdalia:

Okay, the Karate Kid advice has to go. And so do I.

(*Migdalia* walks to her chair and picks up her bag to leave.)

Louisa:

Wait, Migdalia. Maybe we're not asking the right questions.

Migdalia:

Look, I'm not feeling free, and I don't know what's gonna make us feel free, so…

*(**Migdalia** assembles her belongings to leave, and **Alicia** follows suit.)*

Alicia:

I have things to do.

Soledad:

Why were you so excited when you first got here?

Alicia:

I haven't a clue.

Soledad:

We keep talking about what makes us different. What do we have in common?

Alicia:

It's a good thing I didn't pay for this.

Louisa:

Alicia, did you ever wonder why you're not really going anywhere in your career?

Alicia:

I thought you were on my side.

Louisa:

There are no sides here. Things aren't gonna be handed to you. You have to work for everything you want. You came here for a reason. You're gonna leave before you get what you want? Then why bother being here at all? You know, maybe this facilitator is smarter than you think. Maybe this was her plan. She knew we came looking for something. There is something happening to all of us. Maybe she's us. *(pause)* This collective feeling we have, it's what brought us together. Alicia, you said you came here because you had a fight with your manager, but you could have gone to Central Park, you could have gone to Starbucks, to a play…but you came here for a reason. We all came here for a reason.

Soledad:

Okay, so we're here because we want to be free. Can we agree that that's the reason?

Migdalia:

I'm still trying to figure out how "she" is me.

Louisa:

Notice that when we are stuck and when we have questions that there are actual answers here. *(Holds up brochure.)* Well, aren't we the ones looking for the answers?

Maria Elena:

Okay, so you're saying that we will be free when we don't need her or this stupid pamphlet?

Soledad:

I think what Louisa is trying to say is that we can't wait for someone to give us the answer. We have to find it ourselves. No one is going to help us out, if we don't help ourselves out first.

Maria Elena:

This is beginning to feel very surreal.

(Maria Elena sits.)

Alicia:

When you say "freedom," what do you mean exactly?

(Alicia sits.)

Jennifer:

Yeah, free to look the way we want?

(Jennifer sits.)

Louisa:

Well, when you think about it, we have that freedom already.

Maria Elena:

Free to say what we want?

Soledad:

We're in America.

Migdalia:

Yeah, and?

Maria Elena:

We look different, but we want the same things?

Jennifer:

What do we have in common?

Soledad:

Language?

(Soledad sits.)

Louisa:

Only some of us do.

Jennifer:

Barriers?

Louisa:

Again, only some of us do.

(Louisa sits.)

Maria Elena:

Culture? *(looking at Alicia)* Some of us do.

(Migdalia sits.)

Migdalia:

Family.

Maria Elena:

Family. We have a strong sense of family.

Soledad:

Abuelas! Aren't *abuelas* important to us?

Louisa:

Abuela was my greatest teacher.

Maria Elena:

Mine taught me about having faith.

Migdalia:

My grandmother used to kick my ass and then go to her altar and kiss her saints.

Alicia:

Abuela is my biggest source of inspiration.

Jennifer:

I miss my *abuela.*

*(Spotlight on **Jennifer**.)*

Jennifer:

Yes, *Abuela.* I'm listening.

While all my friends were flirting with Javier, the boy that I daydreamed would teach me how to French kiss, I was stuck sitting next to *Abuela* while she gave me a crash course in tortilla making.

I was so restless that I thought my insides would burst. I wanted to go to the mall, but she wanted me to sit and learn. All I could do was sulk and complain, hoping that she would just get tired of it and let me go. I watched the sweat drip down her arm and into the dough, her hands kneading the ball like it was fighting her. "You have to pour the water in a little bit at a time, Jenny, or you have a big sticky mess." Who cares, *Abuela?* I could buy these things in the supermarket, for God's sake. Why spend all this time making something from scratch when it's already made? She looked at me as if she was fighting the impulse to knock me out. Then she would get really angry and start yelling about Utah and Nevada and Arizona.

In the meantime, I imagined my best friend Jordan trying to beat Javier at Gran Turismo, both of them standing so close together scoring while the video game characters pretended to be a distraction for them. The thought of it made me almost sprint out of the house. But *Abuela* scared me sometimes. She kept me sitting chained to the chair with her crazy passion.

I didn't care to know about the old Mexico, the conquistadors and their discoveries. Who cares? I wanted to go to the mall and discover the new Gap shirt that everyone was wearing and I wanted to discover if Javier got tingly the way I did when our arms touched accidentally. Before I could go deep into my fantasy, *Abuela* put the tortilla in the griddle, and she started talking about the importance of real ingredients like sweat and hard work.

I'm gonna scream! I don't understand why she's being so mean to me today. The sun is shining, I'm fifteen, I only get Saturdays and Sundays to play, and she keeps me a prisoner in her kitchen. Why? It seems so selfish and useless, this whole control game she's playing. Finally, we finish making the stupid tortillas and I swear I'll never eat another one as long as I live.

The whole day went by and I never got to see Javier, and I'm sitting with my *abuela* trying to eat so that I won't hurt her feelings. Well, I found out later that Jordan, my so-called best friend, kissed Javier, and he apparently liked it because they became inseparable. I'll always remember that day. *(pause)* Always.

A couple of months later, I came home from school and found my mother crying. She was yelling from down deep inside, and when she saw me she got even louder, like a knife was piercing through her entire body. My father took me aside and he told me that *Abuela* had had a heart attack, and I asked him what the doctors had said. And he put his head down and he choked up, and I knew, I just knew at that moment I would never see *Abuela's* sweat rolling down her chubby arms again. I would never again feel that passion to teach me about the importance of making tortillas from scratch. I would never know why it was such a big deal for her for me to know about Utah, Nevada, Arizona, and the old Mexico. I would never be able to just go and ask her about these things, and in a way, I think, that was her plan, because she left me with the burden and the wonderful gift of finding out myself.

(Lights come up on room.)

Migdalia:

(holding her belly)

Oooh.

Soledad:

You okay?

Migdalia:

Yeah, this little thing is kicking up a storm inside me. *Oye calmate.*

Soledad:

It's been so long since my last daughter. I forgot how it feels to be pregnant.

Louisa:

I'm a little afraid to have a baby. It seems like such a big responsibility.

Migdalia:

It's hard work.

Louisa:

Isn't it amazing, though?

*(**Migdalia** motions to **Louisa** to come touch her belly.)*

Migdalia:

Come here.

*(**Louisa** walks to **Migdalia**, who takes her hand and places it on her belly.)*

Migdalia:

I think about it all the time, especially when the baby kicks. What's amazing is that I have a human being inside me.

Jennifer:

How does it feel to have a baby, Migdalia?

Migdalia:

I'm not gonna to lie to you. The labor is a trip. Right, Soledad?

Soledad:

Absolutely, but it's a wonderful pain. *Mi abuela* used to say, *"Sin dolor uno no puede crecer."*

Alicia:

I'm sorry, what did you say?

Soledad:

Oh, so sorry. She said, "Without pain, one can never experience growth."

Migdalia:

My mother was right, though: the pain hurts so bad that you just want to give up. You want them to take out the baby any way they can. And you're lying there, looking worse than shit on a stick, with your legs wide open and a light as bright as the sun, and you're thinking: why must I be the one to go through this?

And then the doctor says he sees the head. And part of you is thinking: So what? Get it out already! And another part is thinking: Oh God, let the baby be okay. And then in no time, a little human being is lying on your chest looking at you. Crying. Looking for comfort. Looking for love. And you hold it, and you wonder: What did I do to deserve this wonderful miracle? And you realize at that moment that you have no control of anything in this life. As corny as it sounds, having a baby is the best thing that has happened to me. It changes you. It inspires you to do great things. There was a time I thought that women got the short end of everything, but now I know that's not true. Women truly are lucky to be women.

(pause)

Alicia:

I can't have children. Not because I don't want to. Doctor says I can't. So I guess that's why I'm an actress. I can give birth to new lives all the time, right?

(pause)

I remember the first time I watched Rita Moreno in West Side Story. She inspired me. The way she danced, the way she spoke. She was trying to do something. She was trying to tell me something. I wanted to be that. Whatever was making her feel that way, I wanted to feel that too.

Louisa:

When Selena got shot, I actually laughed at that comment that stupid radio DJ made about her. But then I started watching the news reports and couldn't believe how many people she touched, so it made me want to know more about her. I had this idea in my head about what a Mexican was and it was all…wrong. I guess I had my own prejudices. She was amazing. She was just like us; no different. She wasn't just an attractive Latina with a good voice. She was a representative, an ambassador for women. She knocked down barriers so that we could all move a step closer to where we need to be.

Soledad:

For me it was reading a book by Sandra Cisneros. I never thought that I could learn from a Latina from a whole different place. I could relate to her world, even though I'm Dominican and she's Mexican. She made me realize that I still have a lot to learn.

Maria Elena:

My father sits around, afraid to move forward in life. He feels because he has a thick Spanish accent that no one will take him seriously. But he's so wrong. He's so smart and so inventive and so creative, but he's intimidated by the images he sees on television. I don't want him to go through that anymore. I want him to feel he can be anything he wants to be.

Jennifer:

I'm inspired by strength and intelligence, regardless of ethnicity. I am every woman that I've ever read or have been touched by. I am so many women inside this skin. I don't want people to think I'm stupid. I want people to learn from me.

(pause)

Soledad:

Let me be who I need to be.

Migdalia:

Let me be who I need to be.

Louisa:

Let me be who I need to be.

Maria Elena:

Let me be who I need to be.

Jennifer:

Let me be who I need to be.

Alicia:

Let me be who I need to be.

*(**Lisette** enters.)*

Lisette:

Let us be who we need to be, proud Latinas. Can you let us do that?

(Blackout.)

YO SOY LATINA!

✦

(Narrative Version)

The YO SOY LATINA! narrative version, also known as the college version, was written for the colleges and universities who wanted to experience the show but did not have the budget to book the longer off-Broadway version of the play. This version tells the story of how YO SOY LATINA! was born.

Character Breakdown

NARRATOR:

Linda Nieves-Powell's experiences take Latinas on a journey to find their true voices.

ACTRESS ONE:

Lisette Davila Rivera. *Twentysomething wannabe actress/poet*

Migdalia Rivera. *Thirtysomething pregnant Nuyorican married to an African American*

Maria Elena Gonzalez. *Thirty-four-year-old aspiring black Latina actress*

Soledad Tejeda. *Single mom and college student from the Dominican Republic*

Voice. *Casting agent*

ACTRESS TWO:

Lisette Davila Rivera. *Twentysomething wannabe actress/poet*

Alicia Blanca. *Non-Spanish speaking actress from Colombia*

Jennifer Bariquena. *Nineteen-year-old Chicana college student*

Louisa O'Brien. *Twenty-seven-year-old half-Cuban, half-Irish corporate attorney*

Note: Actress One represents all the darker-skinned characters in the play. Actress Two represents all the lighter-skinned characters in the play. Although this version calls for a minimum of three actresses, there have been independent productions that have used six actresses in this version.

Narrator:

Linda Nieves-Powell once heard that if you write down your heart's biggest wish, it will eventually come true. Because when you throw your dreams into the universe, they're supposed to be granted.

All her life she dreamed of finding an answer as to why she was different from everyone else. No one could ever tell her why she was the odd girl out. She needed to figure out who she really was—what her purpose was. So she went in search of herself.

But nobody tells you that trying to find an identity is like trying to climb an oil-slicked mountain. For every step forward, it's ten steps back.

Linda was told she wasn't Latin enough because she didn't speak Spanish. Her Latin friends laughed at her because she lived in a white neighborhood in a big colonial-style house. She wanted to be like them and cut out of school and hang out at the paddleball courts in the projects, but she just didn't fit in.

Her white friends thought she was black because they didn't know what a Puerto Rican was. They laughed at her when she referred to her grandmother as *"Abuela."* Her black friends were some of the best friends she had. They never judged her; they never poked fun at her; they accepted her. But she felt bad, because she couldn't explain to them why she couldn't bring them over to her house. She couldn't explain to them that it wasn't that her parents were really racist, it was just this desperate need they had: to assimilate.

She got so tired of trying to figure out who she was supposed to be that she screamed to the universe, "Please, God, tell me who I am!" He didn't answer her right away. For a minute there, she thought he never would.

Then in 1997, Linda was invited to a barbecue. You don't know when the universe is going to offer you some answers—it just kind of happens to you. Her cousin called to tell her that she had spoken to this big-time Latino attorney about her plays and she thought it would be a good idea to meet with him. So Linda called up the attorney, and he told her he was inviting some local politicians to his barbecue and he thought maybe she could provide some free entertainment in exchange for some free networking. He asked her if she could perform a short piece. She didn't have any short performance pieces, and at the time she wasn't performing any of her own pieces, but the desperate artist in her told him she would.

So she began working on a little monologue that started out with a Latina screaming. The screaming Latina was in a crappy job, and she was really angry about that, because she knew her destiny wasn't in a five-and-dime store. She saw her name in the stars and knew she was meant for bigger things. Her name was Lisette Davila Rivera and she was loud and bold, and because of her, everything came pouring out of Linda—every feeling, every emotion, all the anger, all the humor about being Latina came pouring out of her.

But the pressure of getting this piece done by the weekend was killing her creative flow, and the fear of failure stopped her from going to the silly little networking barbecue. And so the screaming Latina that possessed Linda's body wound up in the bottom of a desk drawer for months—that is, until the phone rang.

An actress friend called to tell Linda she needed material for an audition. Linda told her that she didn't have anything for an audition, but that if she wanted to, she could edit something from her new piece called *YO SOY LATINA!* But Linda didn't think that she'd use it, because it was just so...well, Latino. But she did use it, and Linda thought to herself: *how is she going to walk into an audition with a piece about an angry Latina? She'll never get the part.* Well, the actress called Linda back to tell her that she did in fact get the part and that the person who auditioned her told her that the monologue was amazing. Who would have known? So the actress continued to perform *YO SOY LATINA!* around New York City, and she called Linda to tell her that Latinos were flipping over it. But Linda thought she was just being overdramatic.

Eventually, Linda became curious, and she needed to see the reaction for herself. So she and her actress friend decided to go to Martin Luther King High School in Manhattan to perform it. There were two hundred kids present, and all Linda kept thinking was that they were going to be bored to tears. When her friend started performing, it felt like Linda was on stage with her.

Actress One:

Then fire me! I don't care. But let me remind you, I'm the only one you got that could speak English. Yeah, I thought so, Mr. I-own-one-five-and-dime-store-in-the-worst-section-of-Brooklyn-and-think-I'm-Donald-Trump!

How's he gonna tell me I take too many breaks? Slave trade was over long time ago, Mister Manager!

I ain't no five-and-dime cashier anyway. *Yo soy un actriz.* A future Latina star on the Hollywood Walk of Fame.

I wanna see what you're gonna do when you see me running with the big boys like DeNiro *y* Pacino *y* Garcia.

Actress Two:

I'm telling you: as soon as I get that call…the call that will change my destiny, I'm gonna turn my back, and I'm never coming back.

Keep your broken-down roach-motel tenements and drug-infested ambitions! That's what I'm gonna be yelling down to you fools when I'm on that 747 to LA. LA. I like that. Imagine me, Lisette Davila Rivera, in LA. La La Land, the land of dreams; the place where people play lotto with their lives. I'm gonna be bigger than Rosie Perez, Jennifer Lopez, Salma Hayek, Rita Moreno, and Raquel Welch all put together. I'm gonna be so big that little white kids are gonna wanna be just like me, instead of me having to be like them.

Actress One:

They're gonna want to know how to dance *salsa y merengue.* They're gonna want to eat rice and beans *con chuletas y aguacate.* They're gonna want to watch *Sabado Gigante* for twenty-four hours like any other bored Latino does on a Saturday night.

I'm gonna turn the whole world on to being Latino!

Actress Two:

It's our turn now—our turn to show the world that we're not just little boat people trying to hitch a ride. We got power in our numbers. By the year 2050, Latinos are gonna rule the world! Well, maybe not rule, but we will be occupying a hell of a lot of space.

You're gonna be able to pick up a phone book in Wichita, Kansas, and find a million Juan Rodriguezes. You're gonna find Mexicans, Dominicans, Cubans, Puerto Ricans, South Americans on every inch of this planet. We're gonna be everywhere! They're gonna have to make us the primetime television lawyers and doctors on those stupid sitcoms—instead of the Spanglish-speaking maintenance man.

Actress One:

I want to see my face on the TV set for a change. I want to see my olive skin gracing the covers of *Vogue* and *Elle Magazine.* I want to see my *arroz con pollo* thighs inside the *Sports Illustrated* swimsuit issue, not some skinny little waif with bones sticking out of her back that calls herself a supermodel. Let Kate Moss walk through Orchard Beach in the middle of July without getting laughed at.

Bendito nena, put some clothes on; you look like a human wishbone! What's a body without thighs, without a little bit of *sofrito*? Ah? *Yo soy Latina* and proud of it baby! Nobody's gonna make me feel like an ugly duckling because I'm not anorexic or bulimic.

Actress Two:

This is my body…

Actress One:

…my face…

Actress Two:

…take it or leave it. And that's what I'm gonna say to Steven Spielberg, and I bet you he'll hire me like that. Why? Because I'm not gonna be afraid to be me. That's right! I'm gonna give my people what they've been wanting for a long time. A chance to see themselves. A chance to feel good about themselves. A chance to free themselves from Brady Bunch reruns. That's right. I watched that show for years thinking I had the worst parents on the planet. I never saw Mrs. Brady take a *chancleta* to Marcia's head.

Actress One:

I asked Mommy why she didn't act like Mrs. Brady, and you know what she said? She said, "If you don't like the way we live around here, *vete* and take your father with you!"

So for years after that, I fantasized about being a white child in the Brady Bunch house. I pictured Papi coming home from work and hugging me, sitting me on his lap, and telling me how much he loved me. And how proud he was of me just being his daughter. And no matter what I decided to be when I grew up, he would love me, regardless.

Actress Two:

And then: bam! Reality hits you square in the face. Because the truth of the matter is there is no Brady Bunch existence for Latinos. Forty million strong, and we're still playing the extra in the Drug-Free America public service announcements, instead of the principals in an Ivory Snow commercial.

Kiss my ass!

Nobody is gonna make me do anything! I have the power to be me, not you. I will always be a proud Latina, so that my future son or daughter can grow up confident, self-assured, and proud.

Actress One:

So that they can carry on my love for this beautiful culture of ours, this wonderful array of gifts that have been passed down from our ancestors. A language filled with *sazon*-colored words, exotic foods that feed the hunger of the heart and music…oh, that music…music that makes you stand up and yell…

Actress One and Actress Two:

I am proud to be Latina!

Actress Two:

Custom-made gifts that some of us throw away for the sake of becoming accepted into a culture much colder, much less passionate than ours. A culture that looks at our gifts with a sigh of disgust, for fear it will bring down the value of their communities.

Don't move into our neighborhoods! We don't want you here, unless, of course, you look like us; you act like us; you become us. Forget your past. Join our club. It's free membership! All you gotta do is drain your blood, so there are no traces of history left. Forget where you come from! This is your home now! What more can you ask for?

Actress One:

Well, Lisette Davila Rivera just wants to feel like she's home. That's what I want. So that I don't have to worry about what you will think of me if I'm sitting in my backyard listening to the congas and timbales on the radio while Willie Colón *y* Tito Nieves *y* Marc Anthony make love to me with their voices. I don't want to have to hide my multicolored family from your homeowner's association. *Tio* Hector *y Tia* Juanita can't help the African, Indian, and European blood that runs through their veins.

And neither can I. Let me be who I need to be…

Actress Two:

…a proud Latina.

Actress One:

Will you let me do that?

Narrator:

Linda wanted to cry. Every kid in that auditorium stood up with tremendous pride and started clapping and screaming. It was so overwhelming. It was another moment. She knew that God gave her those words for some reason. She knew that this could not end here, at Martin Luther King High School. This was bigger than her.

But she didn't know what to do with a ten-minute monologue about being proud of being Latina. So Linda did what everyone else was doing: she posted it on the Internet. She logged onto America Online and shared her pride with the rest of the World Wide Web. And then the responses started trickling in.

*(**Actress One** and **Actress Two** read from index cards.)*

Actress One:

Wow, Linda! Where were you when I was growing up? I was so lost and needed someone just like you. With your words, you've made me cry and laugh today. Your words are strong and inspiring. Believe me, there are so many out there that need to hear what you are saying!

Actress Two:

I, too, am a proud Latina. Reading your words gave me the biggest rush. I gave this to my sixteen-year-old daughter, and it bought tears to her eyes, because being born here in the States and the result of a teenage pregnancy to two Latinos (*Boricua* and Mexican), she knows she has Latino blood running through her veins, but never really had been around the Latino community until I moved to Orlando.

Actress Two:

I am a black woman in my early twenties. Your poem was no doubt inspirational to many young people who feel they have to be different to fit into white culture.

Actress One:

I loved your poem! It made me feel even prouder to be the young Latina that I am, and also made me realize how much I don't yet know about my culture, and how I feel that it all gets hidden from me to see, hear, taste, and learn from.

Actress Two:

I want to thank you very much for inspiring me and helping me to continue my writing quest. The poem inspired me to stand up for who I am and what I want.

Actress One:

Wow. That is extremely inspirational. I e-mailed it to every Latina I know.

Actress Two:

Wow, what I just read was so breathtaking. I think more Latinos should speak out the way you or whoever wrote this did. Mad props to you, ma!

Actress One:

I really enjoyed your piece. I am a Latina with all the parts that are considered to be unpretty in American society. But I am proud to be who I am, and I am excited to see one of my sisters out there doing a great job.

Narrator:

The e-mail kept coming in, from across the country and from around the world, e-mail from all different places. And all Linda could remember thinking was: *Wow; I didn't know that there were* Boricuas *in Belgium. Latinos* are *everywhere!*

She received hundreds of e-mail messages from complete strangers who wanted to show their appreciation, and that act of kindness did something to her. She felt that when a complete stranger from miles away takes a moment to pour her heart out to you, you have to pass that love on. And she also knew that no matter how hard this journey got for her, there was no way she could stop. Because she realized, for the first time in her life, that the universe was beginning to answer her questions, and that maybe talking with other Latinas about what they feel about being Latina was in some way going to help her figure out who she was supposed to be.

But she had a lot of work to do, so she starting asking lots of questions and posted a questionnaire on her Web site.

(Actress One and Actress Two read from cards.)

Narrator:

What do you think makes you Latina? Your hair? Your attitude?

Actress Two:

I think what makes someone Latina is her whole sense of being: how she interacts with people and how she presents herself to the world. Just because she has a Spanish last name doesn't really mean she is a *true* Latina. Does she identify with a culture?

Narrator:

What benefits or challenges have you experienced dating outside of your race?

Actress One:

A challenge I have faced is that I am in limbo between being Latina and being white. I was accused of trying to be Latina to make myself more interesting, by other Latinos, or I was considered weird by white people, because I was so proud of my background and refused to hide any inflections in my voice or to change my mannerisms. They assumed that, since I look whiter, that it would be better to forget that part of me.

Narrator:

What do you think are some of the disadvantages and advantages of being Latina?

Actress One:

The stereotypes placed on us. People tend to talk about Latinos as if we are all the same. And it's usually bad! I don't appreciate that, because I am educated. I have a BA and am currently studying for my master's degree. I dedicate most of my time to my family and my community. And I know many people who do the same, and many who are successful. It's not fair how we all have to pay for the acts of others. And the worst part is that we do it to ourselves. I have gotten more slack for being Dominican from people I know than from people I don't. It's so sad that we have people within our own races that defame and judge us. We've heard of Dominicans and Puerto Ricans not getting along. We do the worst harm to ourselves, because others outside our race hear this and then they think it's okay for them to say it. We need to unite and stop the *bochinche!*

Narrator:

After reading their responses, Linda laughed and cried, and she knew something was going on here. Latinas were telling her something that she needed to hear. They were telling her what she had felt all along. In fact, they were telling her something we all needed to hear. She knew that she needed to write a play about all this. She had to write a play to let Latinas know that they weren't the only ones feeling the way they did.

So she immediately went to work. She wrote down an outline of the main issues most Latinas wanted to talk about. Then she internalized everything she had read and sat alone for a while, sifting through the many responses from all the Latinas that were interviewed. She had to find a way to put out all that information together in the most entertaining way possible, and in order to do that, she needed to pull out all the Latinas that were living inside her. It had to come from her heart. She knew it would never work if it didn't come from inside her. And as soon as she put her wishes into the universe, they all came pouring out of her. Six different Latinas were living inside Linda, and it was time to let them out. And for a moment, she thought that maybe after she let them free, we could all be free.

The character Alicia Blanca, an actress who is Colombian, was the first to come to Linda. She came to her after Linda watched an episode of the Carol Burnett show. The episode had nothing to do with Latinos or an audition, but she clearly remembered the structure of the scene. Carol Burnett was playing a character who was trying very hard to get something, and no matter what she did, she couldn't get it; but by the end, she got it her own way. So Alicia Blanca started speaking to her.

Voice (offstage):

Next!

Alicia:

So I look white. What's the big deal? It's just skin color. When I first started going to auditions, casting directors didn't know what to do with me. You get called out to be in a movie like Carlito's Way, they don't expect you to look like this. Instead they wind up casting someone who isn't even Latina, but who they think looks Latina. And what people think I should look like is hysterical. And even more so, the way they think I should speak is even a bigger joke. "Hello Papi, *mira,* I think you're groovy and shit and you know, maybe we can get down or somethin' like dat. Whatchu think, Papi *chulito?*" Can I get a break? I want to be able to tell stories about my people, but they think I don't look typical enough to do that.

Voice (offstage):

Next!

Alicia:

Hello?

Voice (offstage):

Your name, please?

Alicia:

Alicia Williams.

Voice (offstage):

I'm sorry, we are looking for Latin types only. Next!

Alicia:

Excuse me, Casting director?

Voice (offstage):

Please, refer to me as the "Voice."

Alicia:

I'm sorry, Ms. Voice.

Voice (offstage):

No, "Voice." Just "Voice."

Alicia:

Oh, excuse me. I'm a little nervous. Voice, I am all Latina; I can assure you that I am. Really. Don't let the name fool you. I also go by the name Alicia Blanca. Williams is my great-great-grandfather's name. See, he was a German Jew—

Voice (offstage):

Then you are not Latina. Next!

Alicia:

Ms. Voice? I mean, Voice? My mother and father are Latino, really they are. I am one hundred percent Latina.

Voice (offstage):

Can you prove it?

Alicia:

I…I…don't know. I just know that I am.

Voice (offstage):

What is your favorite color lipstick?

Alicia:

Well, I just love lipstick, but if I had to pick one—

Voice (offstage):

Just answer the question!

Alicia:

Neutral Tone by Linda Lee.

Voice (offstage):

Wrong.

Alicia:

Wrong?

Voice (offstage):

The answer is "red." "Red" is what I was looking for.

Alicia:

Okay, if you want me to wear red lipstick for this role, it's no problem. I mean, that's so easy—

Voice (offstage):

No. Next question! What is your favorite television show?

Alicia:

Wow, I mean, there are so many. Well, let me see—

Voice (offstage):

I don't have all day, sweetie!

Alicia:

Sorry. Uh, I would have to say *Frasier*. Yes, *Frasier*.

Voice (offstage):

Wrong!

Alicia:

You don't like *Frasier*?

Voice (offstage):

No, *you* are not supposed to like *Frasier*. The answer was "Telemundo." Next question!

Alicia:

Voice?

Voice (offstage):

Yes, Ms. Williams—Ms. Blanca—Ms. Whatever You Are?

Alicia:

I'm sorry, but Telemundo isn't a show. It's a television network.

Voice (offstage):

Ms. Williams, are you questioning the data I have in front of me? This data was compiled by a group of experts in the television industry. Do you hear that? The television industry. We bring reality into your homes. We take our job very seriously and would never mislead the public. We did extensive research on Layteenas. Are you questioning our expertise in this field, Ms. Blanca...Williams?

Alicia:

No, absolutely not. I wouldn't do anything to jeopardize my chance of being cast in the lead for an all-Latino movie. I'm just saying—

Voice (offstage):

Speak Spanish.

Alicia:

Speak Spanish?

Voice (offstage):

Yes, do you understand English?

Alicia:

Yes! I am fluent in English. But I have to be honest with you. I mean, I should have spent more summers with my grandmother, because I really don't know Spanish that well. *Yo hablo poquito. (laughs)*

Voice (offstage):

Oh, Ms. Williams?

Alicia:

(still laughing)

Yes?

Voice (offstage):

I have been so patient—so very patient, don't you think?

Alicia:

(serious)

Well, I guess.

Voice (offstage):

Ms. Williams, do you know how many Latin women are out there that actually wear red lipstick and speak Spanish?

Alicia:

No, I'm afraid I don't.

Voice (offstage):

They are everywhere! As a matter of a fact, if I looked out my window right now, I would find more than a half a dozen red-lipped, Spanish-speaking, hoop earringed, Spandex-wearing Layteenas. And you know what? I want to find them. Next! Next! Next!

Alicia:

But...but look, Voice. I'm really what you want. I've got passion. I love being Latina. I wear Spandex, sometimes. Really. I want to share that with the rest of the world. I want Latinas everywhere to know they should be proud. My cousin from Jackson Heights wears red lipstick. I mean, I am so perfect for this role.

Voice (offstage):

Listen, Ms. Blanca Williams. Just because I am a casting director does not make me insensitive. But right now I need to find the next big Layteena thing, and unfortunately, you're not it. Thank you for your time. Next! Please send me in the next person!

Alicia:

Wait! Look, all right? I don't know what those cards in front of you say, but I'm telling you, the Latina thing is inside me. It's there. I can feel it. I can't explain it. It's just this amazing feeling of pride about who I am. I love who I am, regardless of my name and the fact that I can't really speak Spanish well. I love that I belong to a beautiful culture that—

(The Voice lets out a big yawn.)

Alicia:

That is so rude.

Voice (offstage):

Excuse me?

Alicia:

That! Yawning like that. You know, maybe the problem isn't me.

(Alicia goes to exit.)

Voice (offstage):

Finally.

Alicia:

Actually, now that I think about it, the problem isn't me. It's those stupid cards in front of you. Those cards are all wrong, Voice. You and your industry don't know anything about "Layteenas." If you haven't noticed, we Latinas come in so many different flavors that Baskin Robbins is planning to put out a new line. I don't want this ridiculous red-lipstick-wearing job anyway. I don't need to put on Spandex to prove that I am a real Latina. Here, I'll prove to you I'm a real Latina, Kiss my *arroz con pollo* ass! Okay, how you like me now?

(Alicia goes to exit again.)

Voice (offstage):

Ms. Williams!

Alicia:

What?

Voice (offstage):

That was a little too stereotypical… *(pause)*…but I loved it! You got the job!

Alicia:

I've got the lead?

Voice (offstage):

You've got the lead. Congratulations, Ms. Williams.

(Alicia runs to centerstage.)

Alicia:

Wow, thank you! Thank you, Voice!

Voice (offstage):

Oh, Voice isn't my real name. It's Ramirez.

Narrator:

Linda spoke to a lot of Latinas who felt like Alicia. Caught between two worlds: the Latin and American world. And then she thought: *white Latinas aren't the only ones caught between two worlds. Black Latinas are too.*

For her, the black Latina was a little easier to create, because she was the "invisible Latina," and she often felt like that. She wasn't a black Latina, but she often felt invisible because she didn't look mainstream. But she didn't know what the black Latina was going to tell her, so Linda had to search deeper for her voice.

While going through some files, she found letters written by actresses who had auditioned for her. In one letter, an actress wrote that she never had any idols. As a kid she always wanted to play Charlie's Angels and she couldn't, because she was too dark. That hit such a nerve, and this inspired Maria Elena—the invisible Latina from Panama.

Maria Elena:

I'm Farrah! I wanna be Farrah, Marisol! Why do I always have to be Kate Jackson? She's so boring! All she does is complain. And I look like Kate Jackson? You look like Bosley, stupid. And I'm tired of you always telling me who I can marry. I don't like the Osmonds, okay? You could have them. They got big teeth anyway, The Jackson 5 are much cuter. Come on, let me be Farrah. I said, I wanna be Farrah!

Marisol:

I said no!

Maria Elena:

That's so not right, Marisol. You're always Farrah.

Marisol:

You can't even do the flip!

Maria Elena:

Oh yes, I can do the flip. Watch me.

(Maria Elena flips her imaginary blond tresses back.)

Marisol:

You don't look realistic.

Maria Elena:

What do you mean, "I don't look realistic"? Forget you, then. There's other superheroes I could be. *(pause)* Aaaah! I know who I can be! I could be *(singing)* Wonder Woman!

(Maria Elena dances around and tries to fly through the air.)

Migdalia:

Your hips are too big.

Maria Elena:

My hips are not big. No, wait, okay? Okay? Don't go! I wanna play "Superheroes"! Wait. Give me a second.

Marisol:

Ooooh. I know who you could be. You could be Fat Albert!

Maria Elena:

I don't wanna be Fat Albert. Just wait; I'm thinking. *(pause)* I got it! Oh, I know who I can be. I can be: Mestiza, Warrior Princess!

Marisol:

Who's that?

Maria Elena:

Well, she's not on any channel, but she's famous. She was this beautiful, strong woman. Part African, part Indian. She had radiant dark skin and large hips. Yeah, but she was beautiful. Yup! As a matter of fact, the boys decided to crown her the most beautiful woman in the village, because no one else looked like her. She was so popular that all the girls were so jealous that they tried to bleach her skin white and straighten her hair. She was a great superhero.

Marisol:

You're making her up.

Maria Elena:

What do you mean, "I'm making her up"? No, I'm not.

Marisol:

You're stupid!

Maria Elena:

You're stupid!

Marisol:

You're stupid!

Maria Elena:

You're stupid. *(She closes her eyes and covers her ears.)* I'm the rubber, you're the glue; whatever you say sticks back to you.

*(She opens her eyes. **Marisol** is no longer there.)*

I wanna play "Superheroes." Don't go…

(speaking to herself)

Maybe I can be somebody else.

(*Maria Elena* *looks into the audience as she pretends to be looking into an imaginary mirror. She touches her hair. She plays with her nose, trying to make it smaller. She looks at the back of her hands, then the front of her hands. After a pause, she returns to the present.*)

Maria Elena:

I didn't have any idols. Everyone told me it was because I was black. I didn't want to be black. I wanted straighter hair. I wanted lighter skin. That little box in my living room told me that I wasn't pretty, that I wasn't normal. I felt invisible. And I still do.

Narrator:

Latinas told Linda that they feel invisible because the media just doesn't get us. They don't know who we really are.

What do you feel about the Latina's image in the media?

Actress One:

Loud, obnoxious, sleazy, and uneducated women who are way too dependent.

Actress Two:

Telemundo programming makes me wanna barf! Spanish magazines continue to be sexist, and the models continue to be photographs of very white Latinas.

Actress One:

Put more Latinos on the American stations so that everyone could see us.

Actress Two:

Until recently, we were only classified as the "the *frito bandito*," or sleeping under a cactus, or in gangs—anything with violence. That's why some of us wanted to be disassociated with our race. We only knew the white men's version of Latino.

Actress One:

There is some improvement, but there is certainly room for more. I am disappointed that some Latinas who are now in the major networks admit they don't speak Spanish. The younger generation who look up to Latinas in the media should know that it is important to become successful, but mastering both languages is key.

Narrator:

Linda always envisioned being able to speak Spanish like the girls in the Bronx speak Spanish, but she knew she wasn't really down like that. But she said that if she had been, her name would be Migdalia and she would say things with a Bronx accent, like: *(exaggerated)* "*Pero mira, Chica, dame la manzan!.*" And sure enough, the character Migdalia came to her. She was a Nuyorican, like Linda. She came from her heart and her soul. She was a little *gordita*, too. But that's okay—Latinas come in all shapes and sizes, right? But she was just like Linda, and like her, she had a little thing for dark men—which caused a lot of hell in her house when she broke the news to Mami and Papi. Linda and her character Migdalia aren't totally alike. They are different in some ways, but the pain is the same.

*(Spotlight on **Migdalia** as she speaks to her mom on her cell phone.)*

Migdalia:

Ma, don't say you don't know. You have to know. This means a lot to me. So let Papi blow a fuse. I don't understand that. I'm Puerto Rican; would it have been okay to bring Bernie Williams home? That's not a different story; it's the same old story. Well, if that's a problem, then we're really screwed. *Ay, screwed* is not a curse. Look, if you want, I'll tell Papi myself; go ahead put him on the phone; I'll tell him. What's the big deal? I'm a grown woman. Geez, what could he possibly do to me? I'm an adult, for God's sake.

Hi, Papi. *Si, estoy bien.* Aha, *pue,* I was just telling Mami that I'm really busy, you know. No, I haven't finished my degree yet, but you'll be the first to know when I do. No, I didn't get that promotion either. Well, corporate America is a funny place, Papi. I do work hard. Well, sometimes it's not about how hard you work, but who you work for. Look, can we talk about this another time? Well, I want you and Mami to meet someone. Who is he? Well, it's not like you know him;

it's just someone that means a lot to me. No, he's not Latino. No, he's not Americano. Well, yeah, he's Americano, but not what *you* think is Americano. No, he's not from Mars either, Papi. Well, remember that movie that you liked about that computer thing? Right! It was with Denzel Washington. Well, this guy I'm seeing is like Denzel Washington. What do I mean? I mean he looks like Denzel Washington. I mean, not totally, but they have things in common. No, he's not a movie star. No. No. *(pause)* Well, yeah; he's a little dark. *(Longer pause.)* Papi, he's African American. What do you mean, "what kind?" There's only one kind. He's black, Papi, like Denzel Washington, Spike Lee black. I don't understand why this is an issue. My kids? When we have kids they will be very loved. What am I gonna cook them? I don't know, food. Like what? I don't know, rice and beans, *pasteles,* macaroni and cheese, maybe collard greens. How are beans and greens gonna make them violent? I'm not doing anything to you, Papi. Excuse me? How can you say that word? You don't remember how kids used to call me that? Well, neither is he. Okay, fine; you don't have to meet him. What matters is how I feel, right? Fine. Nobody's as disappointed as me. Yeah. Bye.

(pause)

How do you think I feel, Ma? This is ridiculous. I never expected this from you and him. Ma, I don't know how to tell you this, but I'm gonna have a baby. Ma? Ma? Then talk to me. Don't tell me you have nothing to say! You have a lot to say. I'm having this baby and I'm marrying him and I want you and Papi to give us your blessings. Ma? Ma, don't hang up please. Mami, don't go! Mami, how can you do this to me? *(Phone clicks off.)* But I do love you.

Narrator:

Unlike Migdalia, Linda was able to change her parent's perceptions of black people. She never thought she'd be able to do that. She says her parents came here thinking one way because their parents came here thinking the same way. Somehow she had to try to change things. Then Louisa, the half-Cuban, half-Irish Latina came to her. At first she came to Linda as a half-Cuban, half-Jewish Latina, but she decided to keep the religious element out of the mix and made her half-Irish instead. Louisa, like all her other characters, was very angry.

Louisa:

We can't erase racism. This country was built on racism. Mariposa was five-foot-ten, she was about 175 pounds, and she was the biggest racist in my high school.

She was Afro-Cuban and hated anyone that didn't want to be like her. And she hated me. Boy, did she hate me. When she found out I was half-Cuban and half-Irish, I heard that she wanted to "fix" me, whatever that meant. We never spoke. She was in special ed and I was in college-bound, so we never had any classes together. She found out what I was because the student newspaper did a story on biracial students.

So I'm in the bathroom stall and I hear the front door open. I smell cigarette smoke, and I see Mariposa's boots underneath my door. She had her two cohorts with her: a girl from Nicaragua that was living with her tenth foster family, and a rich girl from El Salvador who I heard had a crush on Mariposa.

Well, I knew she was waiting for me to come out. So I flush the toilet and pretend that I don't even see her and I walk past her and her gang of misfits. I hear her laughing. So I dry my hands and she says, "Hey, Ms. Half Breed! I wanna talk to you." I didn't even look at her. Look, the girl is an Amazon—I would never win. But I had to do something. So I decided I'd try to outsmart her, and I pretended not to hear her. So she walks over to me and looks me in the face and says, "Did you hear me talking?" So I shake my head no, and I decide to use sign language to make her think I was deaf. So I start doing all these crazy hand gestures, and the Nicaraguan girl says, "I think she's deaf." And Mariposa says, "No shit, Sherlock."

So the girl from El Salvador says, "We could still kick her pretty little ass." And Mariposa says, "How stupid is that? We can't kick her ass if she doesn't know why we're kicking her ass."

And, as luck would have it, the Nicaraguan girl says that she had a foster parent that was deaf and she learned a little sign language while she was there. Now I'm screwed, because I'm not signing with any real communication skill. So she signs and says, "Repeat what you said before." So of course I forgot what I did and I come up with this ridiculous combination of signs I put together from what I saw on commercials and TV shows, and after I was done, Mariposa—who at this point was frustrated as hell because she just wanted to kick butt—asks her cohort what I said.

So the Nicaraguan girl says, "I think she said, 'A sandwich is a sandwich, but the mountain is king.'"

I'm laughing like hell inside, because I didn't realize that I knew that much sign language. Mariposa has this total confused look on her face and asks, "What the hell does 'a sandwich is a sandwich but the mountain is king' mean?" And the Nicaraguan girl just looked at me strange, then said, "I thought that's what she said. I don't know. Maybe I'm wrong."

And at that point, Mariposa took me by my shirt and pinned me against the cold bathroom wall, and she was so close that we practically touched noses, and that made her El Salvadoran friend a little jealous, because she wound up practically on top of us. And then Mariposa asks if I could read lips, and the pain in my throat made me nod yes.

And she said, "Well, let me tell you something. I don't like your attitude. It's a little too uppity and white for this school. If you're really half-Latin, then act like you are."

So I have this vision of me dancing the mambo to prove my cultural pride. I didn't know what to do at that point.

I knew that no amount of mambo dancing was going get me out of this mess. And at that very moment the bathroom door opens, Mariposa lets me drop to the floor, and in walks Sylvia, my favorite security guard.

She asks if everything's okay. And Mariposa says, "Yes," but I don't answer, and Sylvia says, "Hey, Louisa, I heard you were trying out for Maria in West Side Story. How'd it go?"

Paralyzed is not the word to describe what my body felt like at that moment. Then the Nicaraguan girl says, "How's she gonna sing 'I Want to Live in America' if she's deaf?" And it just got deeper and deeper, and I had to speak.

I said, "It went well. Thanks. I'm not sure I'm gonna get it, though." Mariposa looked pissed, and the Nicaraguan girl looked like she saw Jesus rise from the dead. And Sylvia says, "Too bad; they always give it to the white girls."

And suddenly time stopped for me. I stood there between Sylvia, a Cuban mom; Mariposa, another Cuban; a Nicaraguan; and an El Salvadoran; and I never felt so out of place. I thought I knew who I was. So my last name is O'Brien and my father is Irish. I can't erase that part of me, and I don't want to. I know my mother's history, and I love that too. I love that I'm two parts of uniqueness, that I have double identity. But to Latinas, I'm just another wannabe.

Well, the recess bell saves the day, and we all walk out behind Sylvia. I thought I had escaped, but Mariposa and her little gang caught up with me and followed me home that same day and actually did manage to kick my butt. I couldn't fight back. Three against a half was too much for me to handle.

Narrator:

In one word or phrase describe the Latina in you.

Actress Two:

Zesty!

Actress One:

Jibara!

Actress Two:

Driven!

Actress One:

Mamasota!

Actress Two:

Unique!

Actress One:

Vibrant thang!

Actress Two:

The real one!

Actress One:

Orgullosa!

Actress Two:

Compassionate!

Actress One:

Dulce!

Actress Two:

Chiquita!

Actress One:

Pride and beauty!

Actress Two:

Alive and kicking!

Actress One:

Caliente!

Actress Two:

Unbreakable!

Narrator:

What food, visual or smell reminds you of your heritage?

Actress One:

Maja soap and the powder in the bathroom—you know, with that big puffy thing.

Actress Two:

Chili peppers, tacos, and burritos.

Actress One:

Puerco asado and *platano maduros y chuchifritos.*

Actress Two:

Summer barbecues in a tiny backyard with the whole family. And I mean the whole family.

Actress One:

Arroz con gandules, and I can smell *chuletas* from a mile away. Rice and beans and *pernil.* Café Bustelo, *caldos, menudo,* and *barbacoa.*

Actress Two:

When I was little, it was crazy Christmas and New Year's Eve parties until the next morning. Family and friends dancing *merengue* like their lives depended on it.

Actress One:

Leaving grass and water on January fifth for the camels for Three Kings Day back on the Island.

Actress Two:

When we would all go to the beach and loads of family and friends would meet us. Everyone would bring big trays of food, and soda for the kids, and beer for adults. We would stay until the sun went down, laughing, eating, and listening to music. I realized it was a Latin thing because when I went out with my "white" friends and their families, they wore hats, arrived early, brought lemonade, read books, and left early. Very different.

Actress One:

Listening to songs that are only played during the Christmas season: *"Ha comer pasteles, ha comer lechon, arroz con gandules, y ha beber ron."*

Narrator:

Something funny about being Latina.

Actress Two:

That we yell. Why do we yell? We could be sitting right next to each other and we still yell.

Actress One:

Oh, have you ever noticed that Latinos can't say no just once? It's like: "No, no, no, no, no, no," or "No *y* no!"

Actress Two:

The day my mother's friend tried to do *brujeria* on my father because my mother was worried that my father was having an affair. Two days later, he fell down a flight of stairs and crushed one of his balls. My mother never told him the truth, but she never worried again.

Actress One:

Oh, I know. What do Latinos do when a plane lands?

(Both actresses make the sign of the cross, look up to the sky, and begin to clap.)

Narrator:

How did you learn about sex?

Actress Two:

My aunt sat me down when I was fourteen. She noticed I had a small hickey on my neck, and she asked me how I got that. I lied and said I didn't know. I told her I thought I bumped into something. She said, "Well just in case you get clumsy again," and she handed me a condom and a book on birth control methods and told me that a man will tell me anything to get me to page fifteen. So when I read page fifteen, she had circled the man's penis with a red pen and written the words: "The wrong one will ruin your life, but, honey, the right one will too."

Actress One:

Basically, my father sat me down when I was fifteen and he said, "Every time you think about kissing a boy, I can feel it. Every time you get curious about knowing more about the boy, I feel it even more. So if you decide that you want to have sex, I will know exactly when you did it." It took a lifetime to get my father out of my sex life.

Narrator:

The topic of sex was not to be discussed in front of Linda's *abuela*. She said she couldn't even say the word *boy* in front of her.

When Linda was nineteen, she went to spend the summer with her *abuela* in Puerto Rico. She said there were these two guys living next door that were always trying to hit on her, so her *abuela* never let her go out. Any time Linda sat on the porch, her *abuela* would show her the broom, as if to say: *I will knock the living crap out of you if you even attempt to talk to those guys.* She says she hated that summer. But she also said it is one of the best memories she has of her *abuela*. Linda used the memory of her own *abuela* to create Jennifer—the Chicana character.

Jennifer:

Yes, *Abuela.* I'm listening.

While all my friends were flirting with Javier, the boy that I daydreamed would teach me how to French kiss, I was stuck sitting next to *Abuela* while she gave me a crash course in tortilla making.

I was so restless that I thought my insides would burst. I wanted to go to the mall, but she wanted me to sit and learn. All I could do was sulk and complain, hoping that she would just get tired of it and let me go. I watched the sweat drip down her arm and into the dough, her hands kneading the ball like it was fighting her. "You have to pour the water in a little bit at a time, Jenny, or you have a big sticky mess." Who cares, *Abuela?* I could buy these things in the supermarket, for God's sake. Why spend all this time making something from scratch when it's already made? She looked at me as if she was fighting the impulse to knock me out. Then she would get really angry and start yelling about Utah and Nevada and Arizona.

In the meantime, I imagined my best friend Jordan trying to beat Javier at Gran Turismo. Both of them standing so close together, scoring, while the video game characters pretended to be a distraction for them. The thought of it almost made me sprint out of the house. But *Abuela* scared me sometimes. She kept me sitting chained to the chair with her crazy passion.

I didn't care to know about the old Mexico, the conquistadors and their discoveries. Who cares? I wanted to go to the mall and discover the new Gap shirt that everyone was wearing, and I wanted to discover if Javier got tingly the way I did when our arms touched accidentally. Before I could go deep into my fantasy, *Abuela* put the tortilla in the griddle, and she started talking about the importance of real ingredients like sweat and hard work.

I'm gonna scream! I don't understand why she's being so mean to me today. The sun is shining, I'm fifteen, I only get Saturdays and Sundays to play, and she keeps me a prisoner in her kitchen. Why? It seems so selfish and useless, this whole control game she's playing. Finally, we finish making the stupid tortillas, and I swear I'll never eat another one as long as I live.

The whole day went by and I never saw Javier, and I'm sitting with my Abuela trying to eat so that I won't hurt her feelings. Well, I found out later that Jordan, my so-called best friend, kissed Javier, and he apparently liked it, because they became inseparable. I'll always remember that day. Always.

A couple of months later, I came home from school and found my mother crying like she'd had a knife stuck in her back. She was yelling from down deep inside, and when she saw me, she got even louder, like the knife was piercing through her entire body. My father took me aside, and he told me that *Abuela* had had a heart attack, and I asked him what the doctors had said. And he put his head down and he choked up, and I knew, I just knew at that moment that I would never see *Abuela's* sweat rolling down her chubby arms again. I would never again feel that passion to teach me about the importance of making tortillas from scratch. I would never know why it was such a big deal for her for me to know about Utah, Nevada, Arizona, and the old Mexico. I would never be able to just go and ask her about these things, and in a way, I think, that was her plan. Because she left me with the burden and the wonderful gift of finding out myself.

Narrator:

Linda's *abuela* was a strong woman. She knew who she was, and nobody was going to mess with her. She loved who she was. It was her *abuela* who taught her that if you don't like yourself, you've stopped looking for answers. Once you find out how beautiful you really are, then you're ready to fulfill your life's mission. Linda knew she had to create an empowering character based on what her grandmother had taught her, and in walked Soledad, the Latina from the Dominican Republic.

*(Spotlight on **Soledad**.)*

Soledad:

For twenty years, I woke up next to a man who couldn't wash one dish, never did laundry, and couldn't write out his own checks. It was my job to make sure the house was right for him; it was my job to take care of my kids—forget how I felt. Forget about my needs. He wanted sex, you better give it to him. Whether I was in the mood or not, he wanted access.

I wanted access too: to a different life. I used to see other women go to work in the morning, after I took the kids to school, while I walked back into my nice clean house with nothing to look forward to.

I'll never forget the day I decided to leave. The kids were in school. He was home from work. I watched him sitting in his favorite chair. So comfortable; so at peace. He was reading the newspaper. There was a time that watching him made me feel so safe and secure.

I had just finished cleaning the kitchen, and I looked outside the kitchen window, and for a moment, like a sign from heaven, a beautiful little bird appeared on the ledge. It felt like it was staring at me. It just stood there, like I was.

I looked over at Raul. His world so quiet, and mine was exploding. I felt like the ground was opening up under my feet and I had to choose my next step carefully. I looked up at the bird, and it was as if it was looking into my soul, and then it just disappeared into the sky. It was a sign. I know it was.

"Raul. Raul. Can I talk to you?" He put down his paper. Almost like he knew something serious was about to happen.

I sit on the sofa beside him and I say, "Raul, I've been thinking about my life lately. There are things I want to do". He says, *"Dime, que tu quiere."* Men: they think they can fix everything. I tell him I want to go to school, I want to be someone. He tells me I am someone, and goes back to reading his newspaper. I tell him I want to be free, free to experience life. I want to know failure and success. I want to be who I need to be. And in that moment, I saw fire in his eyes, and he slapped me hard against my cheek. There were tears forming in his eyes, and he said, "Soledad, when we got married, we vowed to be together forever. This is something that is sacred to me." I knew it wasn't about sacredness—it was about dependence. He needed me.

Even at that moment, I still wasn't sure of where I was going. My heart was telling me I needed to go; my soul was telling me I needed to find my own way. He cried and asked me if I loved him. I held his head in my lap. I felt his tears rolling down the side of my leg, and I said, "I have loved you, but now I must learn to love myself."

Narrator:

All these six characters, Alicia, Maria Elena, Migdalia, Louisa, Jennifer, and Soledad, left Linda with a wonderful gift that she knew wasn't meant for her only. She knew that she needed to share these women with everyone, so that other Latinas could see that yes, we are diverse, and that makes us a little different from each other—but we still have so much in common.

It was when she realized that—in the greater scope of things—a Dominican or a Mexican is no different from a Nuyorican that her own identity began to take shape. All this time she said she was looking for someone else to give her the answer. She realized that no one gives us the answer. We have to find the answers ourselves. And on this wonderful journey, it has become clearer to her, this vision of being Latina. What makes us Latina? Everything!

THE END

Letters

On behalf of myself and all the sisters of Pi Lambda Chi Latina Sorority at the University of Colorado at Boulder, I extend our appreciation and gratitude for taking time out of your busy schedules to join us all the way in Boulder, Colorado. Your performance and presence *far* exceeded any expectations. We are simply thrilled to have met each and every one of you. I would only hope that the feelings are reciprocated, and you too feel the same about your short but valued trip to Colorado.

Your performance on our campus has been a long time coming...On our campus out of 25,000 enrolled students, at the most 200 self-identify as Latina or Chicana, thus making it seem as though we simply do not exist. But you gave a voice and a face to our stories and experiences; it was a reminder to all who did not realize that we do exist!

Not only did you remind the few present "white" sheltered, wealthy people (90% of CU) that we do exist and we are doing great things, but you also touched on issues that hit a little closer to home. Currently on this campus there is heated tension between the Chicana (Xicana) and Latinas. Issues such as "you're not Chicana enough because you are in a sorority," or "you are not politically active/radical enough." If you are not in Raza Womyn, you are not Mexicana/Chicana enough; you get the point. It is crazy because to have only 200 of us on a campus such as ours, and to have strife and tension, we are only taking ourselves down.

There is so much talk amongst the underrepresented communities on this campus about the "white" conservative males in positions of power, trying to take out all the "minorities" and whatnot. When the truth is: if we don't change our mentality and way of viewing each other, we are going to take each other out without the help of anyone else. However, Monday night I was very pleased to see many women present that needed to be there and needed to hear what was said. Perhaps, and this is my hope, your performance will be the first step in the coming together as a community and allow the healing process to begin on this campus and in our community.

"Yo Soy Latina" hit on many issues that are prevalent in my life as a Latina, and made me rethink what is a Latina, what does being Latina mean to me, and the ways that I self-identify as a Latina. I'm the Latina who has my father's German last name and does not speak Spanish. Yet, I am a Latina, and too often I have felt that I have to prove my "Latinaness" or I'm not Latina enough, all aiding in the personal identity struggle. But one thing is certain after Monday night. I learned that we all have a story; we all have a history and diverse experiences that make us Latina. I do not have to prove being a Latina, just take *my* story and *my* experiences for what they are and know that I am a Latina. Thank you all for a very empowering performance.

—**Renae, University of Colorado at Boulder**

This is one of the six *best* theatrical experiences that I have seen in my entire *life-time*...It is more than just a theatrical experience; it is an eye-opening, heartfelt event. It gently touches on so many nerves in the human societal experience that I think of it as a course in "Society 101"—because it has a much more far-reaching scope than suggested by its perfectly chosen title, "Yo Soy Latina." It addresses every individual's need to find and achieve his/her unique goals in life—within the environment of the multicultural societal influences that sur-round us in our modern world.

—**Theater Mania Member**

On behalf of the Office of Multicultural Affairs and the Hispanic Heritage Coali-tion at American University, we would like to thank you for an exceptional per-formance. Your willingness to open yourselves up so deeply to us has not only been an educational experience for our campus, but has also given light to our AU Latino community.

—**Charla, American University**

The YO SOY LATINA monologue is an honest and empowering piece of art. The students found a means to which they could relate to on a personal basis.

—**Carmen, ASPIRA of New York**

I was touched two years ago when I found the "Yo Soy Latina" monologue online and read it for the first time. When I found out that the Office of Multicultural Affairs was bringing the college version to the campus, I was thrilled! I loved every minute of the performance…These women brought to life six diverse women who had one thing in common…they were all proud to be *Latina!* As a young African-American female, I was touched by the portrayal of six strong women of color who embraced everything that being a woman of color stood for. I was able to identify with each one of the characters in some way, shape, or form. I also had the wonderful opportunity to talk to these three women after their performance and saw that each of them brought some of themselves to these characters. I highly recommend this play to anyone because it has a message that will touch everyone. I look forward to seeing many great things from these ladies who are fulfilling one of life's most important purposes: educating the world and showing people how great it is to be proud of your own rich and diverse culture, whatever it is.

—Jessica, College of William and Mary

Congratulations; the show was great! I took my fourteen-year-old cousin and she loved it. Although I am twenty-six and born in Colombia and she is fourteen and born here, we were both able to identify with the play. It made for a lot of discussion on the way home and with the family at home. Thanks for a wonderful experience.

—Andrea, New York, New York

Thank you SOOOO much for coming to the George Washington University and performing for us.

Race, and just the way we seem to treat each other in this country, has been a big deal for me for a long time. We grow up, most of us do, so isolated originally in our own environments, with no need or opportunity to interact with people of other cultures, or races, or sometimes even political outlooks, that when we do we aren't sure of how to act. Culturally, I think all people have a tendency to associate with what they know as comfortable and normal, and the initial reaction to something new is a sense of apprehension or wariness.

The problem is, a lot of people don't really take that step to grow out of themselves and into the community that surrounds them. Lots of people simply want to stay in their fetal-like lives, never leaving the comfort of their one-view, myopic wombs. The TV says beautiful is this, and the news reports say that bad people have this skin color, or wear those clothes, and most people just don't have the energy to do anything except believe that crap. The outlets and opportunities to really accept and learn about other cultures are very hard to get to given who you are and where you might be, and also are made out to be very scary. I know people who are absolutely paralyzed by the thought of having to think about things outside of themselves—outside the way they normally do. They see no incentive to go and challenge how they think, nor do they see anyone who would care if they did.

I sincerely believe that your show is one of the true pieces of art that will help bridge gaps like these. You simultaneously present an honest and open view of how you see things, and how you see others seeing yourself. Your show is like an open hand and jacket across a puddle, waiting to help someone across, and it's like a little push to get people going.

I was deeply touched by your performance, and I am sure that I cannot begin to imagine what this would mean to a Latina woman.

—**Frank, George Washington University**

The play was absolutely fantastic. The diverse audience that packed the Strauss Performing Arts Center to see your performance cried, laughed, and were inspired as you took them along on a journey that they had not experienced on stage ever before here in Omaha. There was not a single woman who left the hall not thanking me for bringing you to town and telling me she could relate to the characters on stage. You have touched many hearts here in Omaha. Everyone is still talking about you all and your performance. Thank you. I have no words to express what an absolute joy it was for me personally to have you here.

I will be looking for "Yo Soy Latina!" on HBO. That's where you belong. "Yo Soy Latina!" needs to be shown on TV not just once, but over and over again, so the message can reach all. Wishing you all the very best.

—**Maliha, University of Nebraska at Omaha**

I just wanted to let you know that the girls did an *amazing* job. Everyone absolutely *loved* the play. I cannot tell you how many people have asked if we are going to bring them back. Your play has the ability to touch so many people, as I'm sure you already know. Even though I had seen the play before, I enjoyed it and felt that sense of pride after the play, like I did the first time I saw it. I just wanted to let you know that we were very pleased and the girls were so nice. The audience loved them!

—Lisa, University of North Texas

You gave from the heart and it went straight to our own. Thank you so much for giving so much more than a performance—for giving a piece of your heart, your soul, your life; we treasure it.

—Sheila, Diversity Group at World Bank Group

A few hours ago my life changed. I can't believe how powerful your show tonight inspired me. I cried, I laughed and most importantly I dreamed. I saw my vision. I came home and I have not been able to stop writing about ideas and about a storyline in a male's perspective. You have reached women in the most sacred place you can touch them and that is the heart...Remember today, for it is the day I begin on a mission...I will never forget you and your voices! You have shared your life with us; I want to do the same now.

—Jose, George Mason University

0-595-34145-4